MAKING TRACKS

How I Learned to Love Snowmobiling in Maine

TO THE CENTENNIAL LIBRARY—

HAPPY TRAILS ↑
THINK SNOW!

3. 9. 2023

MATT WEBER

Other Outdoor Books by Islandport Press

Evergreens
By John Holyoke

Skiing with Henry Knox
By Sam Brakeley

Backtrack
By V. Paul Reynolds

Ghost Buck
By Dean Bennett

A Life Lived Outdoors
By George Smith

My Life in the Maine Woods
By Annette Jackson

Nine Mile Bridge
By Helen Hamlin

In Maine
By John N. Cole

Suddenly, the Cider Didn't Taste So Good
By John Ford

Leave Some for Seed
By Tom Hennessey

Birds of a Feather
By Paul J. Fournier

These and other Maine books available at
www.islandportpress.com

MAKING TRACKS

How I Learned to Love Snowmobiling in Maine

MATT WEBER

ISLANDPORT PRESS

ISLANDPORT PRESS

Islandport Press
PO Box 10
Yarmouth, Maine 04096
www.islandportpress.com
books@islandportpress.com

ISBN: 978-1-944762-75-9
ebook ISBN: 978-1-944762-84-1
Library of Congress Control Number: 2019931593
Printed in the USA

Dean L. Lunt, Publisher
Book design by Teresa Lagrange
Cover photo by Matt D'Agata: A trail cut on the Maine/
Canadian border.
Back cover photo by Kevin Bennett
All interior photos courtesy of Matt Weber unless otherwise
indicated.

To Mary, who puts up with me always heading off somewhere.
She is my true passion.

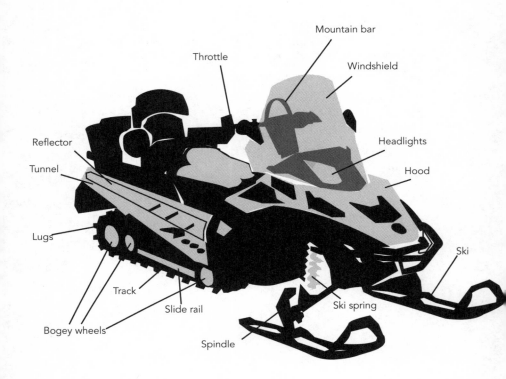

Mountain bar

Throttle

Windshield

Reflector

Headlights

Tunnel

Hood

Lugs

Ski

Track

Slide rail

Ski spring

Bogey wheels

Spindle

Table of Contents

The County

Katahdin and
Moosehead
Region

Sugarloaf

Eastern
Maine

The Western
Mountains

Stillwater

Liberty

Monhegan

Author's Note

I have always been an avid reader and was surprised, and dismayed, to find out that no one has ever written a book about snowmobiling in Maine, as far as I know. This isn't a how-to or a guidebook but rather a recounting of how I got into snowmobiling a few years ago and wound up exploring the entire state. I've separated my rides and adventures into four basic geographic areas: Aroostook County, the state's largest county; the Katahdin and Moosehead region, from Jackman to Baxter State Park; Eastern Maine—the whole of Washington and Hancock Counties, and a chunk of Waldo and Penobscot—generally everything east of Interstate 95; and lastly, the Western Mountains, including the Rangeley Lakes region, Farmington, and Sugarloaf.

I should throw in a few disclaimers:

I would qualify myself as an avid and experienced rider but certainly no pro. Keep in mind that I have only ridden about 9,000 miles on a sled. That may sound like a lot, but there are riders who do more than that in a single season. Indeed, I know of one rider who has ridden more than 200,000 miles in his lifetime. He's been at it for a while—and I've got a long way to go!

I have only a rudimentary knowledge of sleds and how they work. I suppose I am sort of interested in the mechanics behind them, but mostly I want the thing to start up in the morning and keep my hands warm while I'm riding. As the saying goes, I know just enough to be dangerous! After I lost a bogey wheel up in Caribou, I told my wife, Mary, about it like I'd been losing bogey wheels all my life.

Every one of my trips starts at home, on Monhegan. Snowmobiles aren't allowed on the island—nor are all-terrain vehicles, for that matter—but everyone here knows that when the snow is flying up north I'll be headed for the harbor to hop in my boat and steam to the mainland. This boat ride takes an hour one way, and when I get to Port Clyde I'm still an hour's ride in the truck to Liberty and the sleds. So, for me, going for a ride is kind of a process and I try to do my due diligence in regard to weather and trail conditions. It's a long way to come back if the riding is no good.

I almost certainly wouldn't have, and couldn't have, started riding without having the family farm up in Liberty. Everyone there either joins in, or puts up with, snowmobiling. Undoubtedly, it gets old walking around the great heaping piles of gear that are inevitably left in the middle of the most convenient space. Namely the living room.

Matt Weber
Monhegan, 2019

1

The
Beginning

My family has always enjoyed snow. My brothers and I were encouraged to go out and blow off some steam when it snowed. Our winters were full of skis, sleds, snow forts, wet mittens and coats, and epic battles shoveling the driveway. Some adults reminisce about the snowball fights of their youth, but when you're the youngest of three brothers, snowball fights aren't so much fun. Many of us believe that winters past were tougher than today's—darker, colder, and snowier. In fact, winters now are just as savage as they were thirty years ago. Maine still gets massive nor'easters, and brutal shots of cold Arctic air. The sun still sets at four in December. Maybe the one difference is that in this age of digital communication everyone knows what a polar vortex is and when it's showing up.

Just a mile down the road from Orono, the tidy village of Stillwater, Maine, where we grew up, was our winter playground. Our old farmhouse was on a hill that leveled off to a stream, and my brothers and I spent most of our free time on that hill continuously improving our sledding run. The dog was kicked out of her doghouse (which she never used anyway) because we needed to use it as the foundation for a jump. We lugged pot after pot of cold water from the kitchen to ice down the snow until it resembled a bobsled run. Dual slalom courses were constructed, complete with banked sides, although I don't think we ever timed the runs. We'd careen down the chute and then fly off the jump and land in a pile of snow. After a few days without a fresh snow, that landing got awfully hard, I can tell you.

At the very bottom of our hill was a trail that, after crossing a stream, meandered off into the woods for miles. In the spring we got industrious trying to dam the runoff. During the summer we hunted frogs and whatever else moved. Fall was fort building time, and in the winter, once in a while, a loud smoking snowmobile could be seen passing along the trail.

That trail turned out to be a leg of the Great Caribou Bog ski race. Every January, a snowmobiler would come along placing flags and route markers, and the following weekend hundreds of cross-country skiers would come gliding by. The first thirty or so were the serious ones. After watching for a couple of years, my buddies and I hatched a plan to sabotage the race. This we accomplished by digging a massive pit directly in the middle of the trail. I would say it was six feet long and maybe three feet deep. No crevasse, by any means, but it did the trick. The leader of the race that day came screaming around the corner, concentrating on his breathing, saw the hole stretched out in front of him at the last second, and leapt completely over it, landing with a grunt. From our fort, dug fifty yards away under a drift, it was a magnificent effort and we were thrilled with him, and ourselves.

Twenty minutes later two race officials roared up on those old yellow Ski-Doo Safaris and proceeded to shovel the hole back in. (In hindsight, we're lucky no one got hurt.) When they drove off, I watched until they were out of sight thinking how marvelous those machines were, and so too the tracks they left behind. To this day, when I see snowmobile tracks along the side of the road or heading off across a field, I think they're cool. I always wonder who made them and where they were going.

The first time I ever rode on a snowmobile, my mother had set me up for a day with a fur trapper she found through the local fish and game club, so I could tag along as he tended his lines. At that time, I was reading a lot of books about hunting dogs and the outdoors and was convinced that I would probably be a trapper when I got done with school.

It was a Saturday, and he showed up before daylight. Off I went with this fellow who didn't talk much and probably wasn't too keen to have a chubby eleven-year-old boy getting in his way. We drove out past Milford, onto what I now suspect was the Stud Mill Road. In the back of his pickup was a snowmobile. I watched, solemn and wide-eyed, as he backed it off the battered truck and loaded on his gear. On the back of the snowmobile was a metal rack for snowshoes, ax, basket, and the other odds and ends a trapper requires. Then he yanked on the pull cord to start it and that first-ever whiff of two-stroke smoke hit me.

The rest of the day is kind of fuzzy. I do remember never being able to see the traps until we were right on top of them, whether there was something in them or not. At some point we crossed a big stream to retrieve a beaver. During the crossing, I stumbled, and he hauled me up by the scruff of my coat, dripping and shivering. When I got dropped off at the end of the day, I knew that I was not destined to pursue a career of trapping (you know how hard that is?) but that if I could get a snowmobile for next Christmas that would be all I ever needed.

Eight years passed before I sat on a snowmobile again, and it would be nearly a quarter of a century before I purchased one for my own use.

In the fall of 1994, after a mostly unremarkable career at Old Town High, I deferred my acceptance to the College of the Atlantic in Bar Harbor. I visited the job fair at Sugarloaf Mountain, landed a job with the snowmaking crew, and lucked into a bunk room of a condo owned by one of the ski instructors. Sugarloaf is the second highest mountain in Maine, and the largest of the state's numerous alpine skiing operations. I had learned to downhill ski there years before, and although I never anticipated working there, snowmaking turned out to be the one job that has outshone all the others as the favorite thing I've done to earn money. I was put on the weekend day shift: Friday to Sunday, 9 a.m. to 9 p.m. one week, Thursday to Sunday 9 a.m. to 9 p.m. the next. Days off, I skied.

My boss, Danny Barker, was a local from nearby Stratton who had been blowing snow at Sugarloaf since *he* was out of school, and he knew the mountain inside and out. One of his favorite tricks was to meet one of us at the top of say, the Skidder trail, offering to take your gun run for you if you could knock him off his feet. This was tempting to us snowmakers because gun runs were, and still are, the bread and butter of the job. Twelve-hour shifts of trudging down, and sometimes up, those long Sugarloaf trails, manhandling snowguns and digging out snow-covered hoses is a long day's work, and it was tempting to see if the boss could still hack it.

Of course, he could. He spent more time on that mountain than probably any other person alive. Danno was maybe five foot eight, and years of working on the steep trails of Sugarloaf had left him in deceptively good condition. After a few attempts (*I mean, how tough can this old guy be?*), I realized I was outmatched. I'd charge through the snow at him, looking to drive a shoulder into his stomach, and just as I was making contact he'd deftly sidestep and thwack me on the back of my helmet while simultaneously sticking a foot out, and I'd plow headlong into the snow. His low center of gravity was ideal for the task, and he knew it. I'd start my gun run down the trail listening to him laughing as I wiped snow off myself. To my knowledge no one ever did manage it, and we were some pretty big boys ourselves.

It may seem hard to believe, but the powers that be on the mountain never gave the snowmakers any new equipment. Usually the latest and greatest machines were reserved for the lift mechanics or the head ski patrol. They did not, apparently, have a reputation of being hard on equipment. We snowmakers were used to being considered a second class of mountain worker and worked carefully to keep it that way. At various times, for various parts of the mountain, we used four-wheelers, snowmobiles, and groomers to move miles of hose and snowguns from one trail to another. This was all part of the allure, of course. The thrill of roaring *up* a black diamond at Sugarloaf on a snowmobile is really just as good as roaring *down* on skis. The motley collection of beat-up old sleds delegated to us included short tracks, fanners, old lake racers and the like—basically, all the sleds that have no business working on a mountain. We invariably got halfway to where we needed to be and the thing would sputter to a stop as the aged engine overheated. Often some hapless snowmaker would bury the thing four feet down a drifted-over water bar and this was where

Danno's life in snow country truly came into play.

The radio call went something like this:

"Ahh, 404 from 421?" (Danno is 404, and I'm 421.)

"Go ahead, 421."

"Any chance you're somewhere near the top of Flume?"

"Why?"

"Well, this stupid Jaguar is buried and then I overheated it trying to break out and it won't start."

"How buried is it?"

"Worst I've seen. Bottomless."

"Gonna cost you if I can get it out by myself when I get there."

"Yup."

You can guess what happens next. Danno roars up, shakes his head, calls you any number of names beginning with *amateur* and ending with *numbskull*, gets on the miserable old Jag, which naturally starts first pull for him, and is back out on the trail in about 0.3 seconds.

"That's going to be a twelve-pack, Weber."

"Wait, I thought it was a six-pack?"

"Nope, it's twelve. That's the third time this week."

It didn't matter that I was eighteen and couldn't legally buy beer. I probably never did get him the beer, and he probably never cared that I didn't. For Danno, the fun was coming to bail his guys out of whatever trouble we got ourselves into on the mountain—and believe me, it was a lot.

One of the lousy aspects of snowmaking was that the day after a big nor'easter blew through the snowmakers would have to go shovel all the condos out. There was a lot of bellyaching about this because we all wanted to ski the fresh powder on these days. I remember one of us, at twenty-five years old or so a veteran snowmaker, was given the job of driving some equipment around for the racing program in a brand-new long track Skandic the morning after one of these storms. This task had him bitching something awful about missing the best ski day of the year, but away he went. After about eight hours of shoveling roofs we were dismissed and met up with the guy on the Skandic as he was finishing his day. He was grinning from ear to ear while we were sweat-drenched and sore from shoveling. Turns out driving a brand-new sled can be a pure delight, especially a Skandic that is ƒbuilt for deep snow. He informed us that he had had a great day, the sled would go anywhere, and oh, how was shoveling?

After February, Maine's Western Mountains usually have eight or nine feet of snow and there's no call for daily snowmaking. The crew chiefs and their crews are summarily let go with the exception of a skeleton crew kept on to blow a little fresh ice for a big ski race or snow to cover the red spot if one of the groomer drivers shoots a moose on Tote Road. I asked to be a part of this duty and was chosen. For some reason Danno took a liking to me and a couple of other guys, and this was the group that stayed on.

One day he asked me if I'd be interested in side work shoveling roofs at some remote fishing camps owned by friends of his. It was a twenty-mile ride in by snowmobile, lasted two nights, and we were paid ten dollars an hour and all the food we could eat. After considering the offer for nearly half a second, I said yes.

To this day, I am still looking for these camps. Every year I run into Danno at the mountain and I forget to ask him where they are, but that was my first experience being in the true backwoods of Maine. I couldn't tell you exactly what we ate, but it was the finest food I ever remember eating. Shoveling all day will help an appetite.

It was the classic Maine setting, too—a small river mostly frozen with a few open spots, low-slung cabins with smoke hanging around the yards, various antlers on display over every door, porches walled in with snow. I couldn't tell you what sleds we rode in on, and I doubt we had helmets, but the trip was nothing short of magical.

But as fun as Sugarloaf was during these years, it was a winters-only job for me. Summers I spent on Monhegan Island. These summers turned into spring, summer, and fall and, finally, I moved there year-round. I discovered commercial fishing and quickly fell in love with life offshore, be it boat or island. Lobstering on Monhegan is mostly a wintertime activity, and soon enough snowmobiles were the farthest thing from my mind. Instead, I fished. I spent the colder months catching lobsters around Monhegan, and the summer months I roamed the Gulf of Maine, chasing tuna, herring, scallops, or whatever else seemed interesting. I'd often be gone for weeks at a time, coming back sunburned and heartsore for my island. I had nothing tying me to home and was free to do as I pleased (as long as the rent was paid up). Whole years would pass during which riding a snowmobile never occurred to me as realistic. It wasn't until I met my wife that this would change.

In 2009, I met Mary, and we knew on our third date that we were meant for each other. I convinced her to visit Monhegan, and she too fell in love with the island. A year later she said yes when I asked her to spend the rest of her life with me. So, newly married, in a modest house that I had built five years earlier on nearly an acre of land (which is a lot on an island), owner of a rugged little lobster boat, and possibly even showing signs of maturity, I was often looking around with a sense of personal satisfaction.

I am lucky to get along famously with Mary's family. Her parents,

Dan and Carol McGovern, have an old farmhouse on top of a ridge in Liberty. This interior Midcoast is a wonderful part of Maine. Essentially, it's a series of ridges and valleys, dotted with lakes and ponds, and a few important rivers. The house and one hundred acres sit mostly on blueberry barrens and overlook Lake St. George. It's a good wholesome life up there on the ridge, particularly if you like the wind.

The first time I ever visited that house, for the "meet the parents" dinner, Dan had a particularly tasty, and particularly strong, double IPA on tap in the kitchen. I didn't know that night of Dan's history with craft beer in Maine, that he had been brewing professionally since 1992, and that he would, a few years down the road, teach Mary and me the finer points of the business. I also didn't, at the time, know what a double IPA was and certainly wasn't aware of the alcohol content. I didn't know Dan well enough to be wary when he insisted on pouring me yet another pint from the tap in his kitchen, nor did I know enough to recognize the gleam in his eye as I innocently accepted it. I just thought, *eh, beer is beer, and I'm a rum drinker . . . no problem here.* It wasn't long into the evening before Mary was elbowing me in the ribs trying to get me to clam up. That IPA was tasty and having it on tap next to the kitchen faucet was making it too easy to indulge. Before too long, I was offering up advice at the table, free of charge, to anyone who would listen. Luckily, her family is about as friendly as they come, and they just shrugged it off, probably wondering how such a stumbling, rambling fool stayed alive fishing for lobsters all winter.

Several years later, I was helping Dan get his winter's supply of firewood bucked, split, and stacked, when I noticed an old clamshell snowmobile trailer sitting back among some alders behind his wood-

Dan, Mary, and me in front of our brewery, Monhegan Brewing Company.

shed. I asked him about it and he said it was full of Mary's old furniture. With a little more prodding—getting information out of him isn't always easy, particularly when he's working—I discovered, to my absolute delight, that in fact Dan was a snowmobile fanatic, had previously owned more than a few, had ridden all over Maine and also the Gaspé Peninsula, still had all the gear, and, though he didn't come right out and say, missed it. So, while we split and stacked wood we talked about snowmobiles, and I grilled him about where he rode, what kind of sleds they were, and what it was all about.

Steaming the boat home from that weekend in Liberty, I had something new to think about, a topic I hadn't spent much time dwelling on for many years. I realized I could conceivably justify buying myself a snowmobile. For years, I had put all the money I earned back into my fishing business and then into our house. I wouldn't get a new sled, I mused to myself, but maybe an old beater would be just the thing. Moreover, I wouldn't have to worry about what to do with it when I wasn't riding. I could leave it in Liberty. It's a twelve-mile steam from Port Clyde to Monhegan, and by mile three I had convinced myself it was probably a great idea.

Now, most people, particularly in the online age, would spend hours and days on their computer or device researching the best deals, reading the specs of, and discussing the merits of, the plethora of snowmobiles that are on the market today. There are four major brands. In no particular order they are Ski-Doo, Yamaha, Arctic Cat, and Polaris. These four companies break down sleds into various categories: trail sleds, work sleds, race sleds, mountain sleds, and crossovers. Each company makes something for everyone, and, like Ford and Chevrolet trucks, each company has its champions.

Normal folks would know exactly what they wanted in a snow-

" **Long tracks, with skis closer together, are better for ungroomed backwoods trails. Sleds with shorter tracks, with skis farther apart, give you better handling on groomed trails.**

mobile. For instance, that trapper who took me along for the day would want a longer, wider track so he wouldn't get stuck while checking his trap line, and, because it would almost always be off of the groomed trails, he would also want something with the skis closer together for winding through brush and trees.

If you were looking to put on as many miles in a single day as you could, a sled with a shorter track and wider ski stance would give you greater handling on groomed trails and would often have metal picks in the track for added traction on icy trails, similar to a climber's crampons.

Naturally, I didn't know what I wanted a sled for, other than fun, didn't even know I had options, and certainly wasn't about to spend any time doing research. I just knew it would have to be under $2,000, the limit I had set for myself. Dan and my brother-in-law Jeff both knew I was looking, though, and soon I was getting texted Craigslist ads for all sorts of sleds, mostly out of my budget. When I finally did settle on one, the criteria were basic. It was less than an hour's drive from Liberty, had relatively low mileage, and the man only wanted $1,900, although I was able to go less when I offered all cash, in true lobsterman fashion. The first sled I ever owned would be a Yamaha, a 2004 SX Viper, which Dan called a lake racer. Lake racing is a common thing among snowmobilers, as frozen bodies of water are often smooth and offer long stretches of high mph opportunities. These sleds are built for speed.

Jeff and I took off one Saturday morning and after a few wrong turns found the farm in Monmouth. An older gentleman came to the door and I explained I was the fellow who had called about his old snowmobile. We walked over to the ditch where he had left it and he explained, in an uninterested way, how to start it. I was pleased to see it started up and I nodded approvingly, inwardly wondering how the thing worked and if all snowmobiles smoked as much as this one was smoking currently. We loaded it into the back of my truck and off we went. I remember thinking how big that Viper looked in the rearview mirror. It seemed kind of vicious with its black and silver accents, and that smoke was just as intoxicating now as it had been when I was ten. Upon our arrival back in Liberty, Dan came to have a look. There was a lot of hemming and hawing, looking at the engine, track, picks (*oh, those are picks?*) before he pronounced it a decent sled, for its age.

"Those engines are bulletproof. That'll be good, for someone like you." I was left to consider this as Dan stalked off to his tractor, but in truth, I think he was a little jealous. It had been some years since he had sold his snowmobiles and I know he missed them.

That was the middle of October 2013, and of course it didn't snow for two months. Along about Thanksgiving I started watching the weather with an eye out for snow rather than a good day to haul traps. I didn't have to wait long. One Friday, Mary and I were in Liberty, the Viper waiting patiently in basically the same spot I had left it, and six inches of new snow on the ground, without a track on it. The family knew we were coming for the inaugural trip for the Yamaha under its new ownership.

They waited as I looked for my old skiing pants, then jacket, then watched as I tried on one of the old helmets for the first time,

My first sled, a 2004 Yamaha SX Viper.

fiddling with straps, trying and failing to open it. Exasperated with the stupid helmet, I told Dan he might as well go for a spin while I frigged around. After waiting for approximately half a second, he hopped on the idling machine with no gloves, no helmet or even winter hat, and rolled off to the edge of the field.

By this time, I had managed to squeeze the helmet on but couldn't see through the sun shield that was down and, apparently, was only able to be manipulated by a Rhodes scholar. I was finally able to drive the shield up in time to see Dan, by this time possessed of a wild gleam in his eye, hunched over the sled, head ducked just below the windshield and rear end sticking out behind him in true race fashion, squeeze the throttle open all the way and roar off across the field. We all watched, fascinated, and then cheers and laughter erupted as he approached the far end, turned around, and screamed back toward us, snow flying up behind the sled in a great rooster tail.

I thought you had to warm these things up, I wondered, thinking of the big diesel in my boat. That field is about five hundred yards long and the same wide and it was clear to all of us that he had hit, at minimum, seventy miles an hour. I never knew sleds went that fast, but then again, there were a lot of things I didn't know about these machines.

That afternoon I laid tracks all over that field, across the road, over the ridge, pretty much anywhere I could get the sled. I had come to an agreement with my helmet and had a wonderful time. Carol, Mary, and Mary's sister Elizabeth (Jeff's wife) quickly tired of the fun and retreated to the house and heat. Dan and Jeff and I followed a little while later. Over cold pints of beer and dinner, the discussion was all about snowmobiles. I listened raptly as Dan told of previous exploits and trips to places that I had only vaguely heard of. If you've ever heard someone talk about a passion that they haven't pursued in some time you may know how that evening went. There was a certain wistfulness to his words, of times up in the North Woods with friends, cold wood smoke and church towers rising above snow-filled valleys, trails wide and flat, and trails steep and treacherous. I took it all in, slowly starting to realize that now I had my passport—in the form of a Yamaha Viper—to explore all regions of Maine. The possibility of just going across the lake to get a slice of pizza also wasn't lost on me.

I wasn't the only one who heard Dan talking that night. Carol also heard the tone in his voice and knew it for what it was. She had accompanied him on a fair number of snowmobile trips and at one point they each had a sled. The next day she took Jeff and me aside and asked if we thought there might be a used sled to be found for Dan, and would we go get it when it was found? She had decided to get him one for Christmas that year. After I had left my snow-mobile basically in their front yard that fall, Carol had noticed her husband looking on the internet at used sleds and muttering every now and then about the relative merits of two strokes versus four strokes, getting the old trailer registered, and which company had the best spring check deal.

Before long we had narrowed it down to a family friend's used Ski-Doo, and Jeff and I departed one morning to retrieve it. The plan was to drive up to Moosehead, load the sled on my truck and have it back to Liberty, safely hidden away in the trailer, before Dan got home from work.

Sounded simple, and it should have been. Arriving in Green-ville after a two-hour drive we marveled at the three feet of snow on the ground. We had no trouble finding the house, tucked a few miles back from the paved road, and managed to open the garage using the pass code the owner had given us. So far, so good. Jeff, being far more mechanically inclined than I am, managed to get the big red Ski-Doo started, turned around, and pointed toward the driveway. (We had concluded, erroneously, that this particular sled did not have reverse.) We spent the next hour zipping around the driveway, the road, and the yard trying to get the sled perched atop a snowbank. Our plan was to drive the sled down the snowbank and into the bed of the truck. We finally managed it after getting stuck four or five times and were thoroughly worn out. Snowmobiles have a way of doing that sometimes, leaving you bewildered, ticked off, soaked through with sweat, and wondering when the fun part is going to happen because this is nothing short of stupid.

Unloading Dan's Christmas present back in Liberty took a minute. It wasn't pretty, and it probably wasn't easy on the machine, but we were well past caring by then. Into the trailer it went, and we used my Viper to cover the different track patterns left by the Ski-Doo, in case anyone, like our father-in-law, was onto us.

Two days later, Christmas morning mayhem about done, there remained only one small, heavy box left under the tree. We all knew it was for Dan and what it was for. Jeff and I had concluded, correctly this time, that the Ski-Doo's battery was junk, so Carol decided instead of wrapping up a snowmobile and trying to get it under the tree that she would just wrap up the new battery. Someone handed the last box to Dan and he opened it.

"Ahh, good," he said politely. "I was thinking about getting one of these."

"Dan, that's for your snowmobile."

"Wull, I don't have a snowmobile."

It still had not dawned on him.

"You do now. It's out in the trailer!"

And out we all marched to marvel at the big red Renegade that had given Jeff and me so much trouble. Dan took it all in stride, but we could tell how much it meant to him. He spent the rest of the day taking it apart in the heated woodshed, engrossed with learning it inside and out, figuring how they put it together, changing the chain case oil, greasing everything, wiping away the years of grime. Basically, doing everything that never occurred to me to do when I got mine.

That was the beginning. Suddenly all of Maine lay just outside the door, waiting for a couple of old snowmobiles from Liberty to show up. And we would, in the next few years, visit almost every corner of the state. It would take me a few years and a lot of miles to finally find the right gear to ride in and, eventually, move up to a new sled, bigger trailer, and most importantly, a better understanding of snowmobiling. I knew it would be great fun, but what I didn't realize was how many wonderful folks I would meet, in every town I went through, who all shared the same love of Maine, and winter, and snowmobiles.

2
Learning to
Ride Right

For the novice snowmobiler, there are a wide range of matters concerning the sport that are handy to know. I can attest to this because I knew none of them that first winter with my Viper. Trails and trailers, helmets and other gear, riding etiquette, navigation, weather, basic knowledge of engines and fuel—the list goes on. Of course, many of us grow up learning about some or all of these things. Living in Maine promotes an awareness and practicality that most other states don't require. In fact, being a true Mainer is a badge of honor and usually a sign that one is possessed of large amounts of logical thinking and hands-on ability.

Due to a technicality, I can't call myself a true Mainer. Though my parents were living in Kittery at the time, I was born across the river in Portsmouth, New Hampshire, approximately one hundred yards from the border. I am still trying to come to grips with this. I have managed to become self-reliant and competent (to a degree) and have also learned that while many situations call for clear thinking, experience, and cleverness, many also require nothing more than a strong back. This is certainly true for snowmobiling, and you'll thank that strong back of yours the first time you bury your sled in a drift somewhere and have to muscle it back on the trail.

Trails and Trail Maps

Maine is crisscrossed with some 14,000 miles of snowmobile trails and they are broken down in several ways. The biggest trails are the Interconnected Trail System (ITS) trails, and they cover nearly every corner of the state, including extreme southern Maine where ITS 89 starts its meandering way north just a few miles from New Hampshire. Through a joint effort between the Maine Snowmobile Association and the Snowmobile Division of the Maine Bureau of Parks and Lands, every year an updated map of ITS routes gets published. Often, the routes change according to landowners' whims or logging operations, so you do need a new one each year.

These ITS trails are almost always the widest, best-marked, most frequently groomed trails you can choose to ride on. The state funds nearly one hundred snowmobile clubs, subsidizing their equipment and fuel needed to run the groomers, but these clubs—and the many others in the state—also rely on memberships and fundraisers to meet their budgets. Many of the clubs are responsible for maintaining and grooming miles of trails, and it is common for a groomer operator to spend ten hours a night grooming forty or more miles of trails, five or six nights a week. This is mostly done on a volunteer basis by talented and dedicated fans of the sport. Riding the ITS, it is common to cover two hundred or more miles in a day, and if you have the proper registration these trails can take you to New Hampshire and then Vermont going west, or north and east to New Brunswick and on to the Gaspé Peninsula.

Many towns have local "club" trails, and these generally are not quite as wide and may be less frequently groomed. They have fewer straightaways and wind in and around towns and the local ponds and streams. Sooner or later many will connect to an ITS trail. Local trails are commonly bumpy and not always well signed. I have often taken the Liberty trails and become thoroughly turned around or dumped out on some plowed road I'd never heard of. If you've grown up on these trails it's no big deal, and to be honest some of my best rides happened precisely because I was lost and discovered some magnificent view that no one had visited in months or even years. Just make sure you turn around and follow your track home before you've used over half of your tank of gas or else you'll be leaving that wonderful machine where it ran out of fuel and looking at a long walk through the woods to the nearest gas station.

Going out on an unmarked trail? Make sure you turn around and follow your track home before you've used over half of your tank of gas.

There are almost always trail maps for whatever area you choose to ride in, and you are highly encouraged to bring these along. Many clubs create a trifold of their area complete with trails, mileage, gas pumps, scenic views, warming huts, and likely spots for lunch. By the end of each winter the cab of my truck is littered with trail maps from all the areas I've ridden. Coupled with the state ITS map, you should be able to navigate your way to nearly any place you're likely to go. If you're not too confident about determining which way is north, throw a small compass on your key chain. When I'm taking off for a new area, I'll also bring along the backwoods bible known to Mainers as the *Gazetteer*. *The Maine Atlas and Gazetteer* has seventy-plus pages of in-depth maps of the entire state, and I suspect it is one of the most thumbed-through publications in Maine.

My most recent purchase was a GPS unit that mounts below the windshield and has a nice screen that shows roads, trails, and topography. It shows where I've ridden so far that day and thus allows me to reverse my course back to the beginning of the ride. Normally, I'm confident in my ability to navigate—likely because of my life on the ocean. In fact, having that little GPS on the sled reminds me of being on my lobster boat with its chartplotter, marking where I've set all my traps. Kind of homey.

The *Gazetteer* or a GPS is also helpful when you're chasing the snow conditions. Often in the beginning of winter it's necessary to trailer the sleds to a part of the state that has enough snow to ride. It's very common to see a line of trucks and trailers pulled over on the side of some logging road north of Rangeley and snowmobile tracks heading off down a side trail. The early-season riders who are willing to drive their truck 150 miles just to be able to drive their sled fifty are likely the best overland navigators in the state, second only to the loggers and woodsmen who are in the backcountry year-round.

Weather Forecasts

In the modern day of smartphones and radar, websites full of computer weather models, and updates via social media, being on top of the snow and weather conditions is easier than ever before. The fact that this data is all so readily available in no way diminishes the need to know it. On my phone I have five weather apps, both ocean and mainland, and I also look at several websites that provide real-time weather forecasts, current radar updates, and the latest run of four different weather models. On social media I follow a number of snowmobile clubs and weather services. These folks constantly update the weather and trail conditions, as well as the ice thickness of rivers, lakes, and ponds.

When I plan a ride or a trip, the first thing I look for is snow depth. The next thing I want to know is what sort of conditions I can expect to have during the trip. Will it be sunny and windy? Is there a big nor'easter moving in? Was there recently fresh snow or rain? How will any of that affect the day's ride? If the high temperature for the day is only going to be ten degrees I know I need to bring more layers or I'll be freezing my butt off all day.

One day, early in March, I left Jackman with a buddy and rode to Northeast Carry at the top of Moosehead Lake. This township, at the top of Maine's biggest lake, is a common rest stop for snowmobilers in the winter and a hub for summer campers and canoers. The temp when we left was three degrees and we had a fresh three inches of light fluffy snow from the night before. No big deal, and I barely noticed the wind was cranking along about thirty mph or so. (It's easy to forget about wind when you're riding along at fifty mph.) We were pretty chilly by the time we got to Raymond's Store and fueled up, and I was thinking about having a nice burger in front of the fireplace at a little spot I'd been to the year before. The Birches Resort, on the west side of Moosehead, is prime lakefront property and offers up stunning views of Mount Kineo sitting a mile across the water. They also serve up a terrific lunch. Thinking I'd knock off fifteen miles of the ride, we followed some tracks out onto the lake and headed south toward Mount Kineo's sharp, towering cliff.

Once out on the frozen expanse of Moosehead Lake, that wind, which I had thought nothing of before, was free to do its thing, and its thing this day was creating a stout ground blizzard with that fresh snow. Visibility and windchill dropped the farther we went and suddenly we could only see thirty yards ahead of us. Just visible over the whiteout was Kineo, out ahead of us some ten miles down the lake. Behind me I could see the headlight of my friend's sled

"Wind and snow can combine in unexpected ways. What appears to be a nice sunny day can change quickly depending on where you are. Most of the time, shortcuts are just not worth it.

bouncing in and out of sight as he followed in my track, probably wondering what in the world was wrong with sticking to groomed trails in the woods. It wasn't long before we hit a few small pressure ridges and we slowed down again to keep from getting tossed off the sleds. The hazard of hitting one of these at speed, or running into a stretch of open water, dawned on me. Even in the coldest winters there are parts of that lake that don't freeze. At some point I decided that turning around was just as sketchy as going forward, so we kept on, going slow and following the drifted over tracks ahead of us.

We made it, but it was nerve-wracking and at times just plain scary. Most of the time, shortcuts are just not worth it.

This incident was an important lesson for me. First, what appears to be a nice, albeit cold, sunny day can change pretty darn quickly depending on where you are. Had the ground blizzard been just a few feet higher off the ice, I would never have been able to see Kineo and thus keep my bearings on the lake. Take the wind or the fresh snow out of the equation and we wouldn't have had any issue, yet with my relative inexperience it never occurred to me what we would encounter in the open with the two combined.

If we had run out of gas we would have been on foot, in a blizzard, on a lake, with no one knowing where we had ridden that day. Most importantly, I believe, was that we were following old tracks without having talked with the locals about the latest ice conditions. Just because someone went across there first doesn't mean it's safe for others to follow. We were lucky, and the lesson is that you can't depend on being lucky. Being on top of the weather and snow conditions and anticipating the impacts doesn't guarantee your safety, but it sure does help.

Besides the weather that day on Moosehead, we could also have run into trouble mechanically. The track of a snowmobile is run by a belt—when you squeeze the throttle, the engine revs and in turn engages a clutch that then turns the drive belt that, through a set of gears, turns the track.

Some riders can tell you all about the gears and clutching on a sled, but I'm not one of them. I get by because I have my sled serviced every fall by professionals. It's one thing to comprehend the basic principles of small engines and another thing entirely to diagnose and repair them. I was lucky with my first sled. Dan was right when he said the engine in that old Viper was bulletproof. I have never had an issue with it, and we still run it to this day.

I did once blow the drive belt on it, going down one of the famous rail beds in Aroostook County. These unused train tracks are great fun if you like going fast. They are straight and flat. That day I was blasting along at about eighty mph (trying to keep up with Dan) when I looked down and saw what appeared to be the remnants of a white bird on my left knee. Then the sled lost power and rolled to a stop. Upon opening the cowling, I saw the shredded remains of the drive belt and realized that I hadn't hit a bird at all. The belt, as it was disintegrating, was shooting out white rubbery streamers that resembled the tufts or feathers of a seagull. Sooner or later everyone will blow a belt, and though it's not too difficult to replace a belt, I recommend practicing it someplace warm before you have to do it in the cold woods. Having a certified sled shop inspect and overhaul your snowmobile is a good idea. I personally couldn't tell you if your Hyfax are worn out, or if

"

I get by because I have my sled serviced every fall by professionals.

the bogey wheels have been greased lately, but I'm sure those things are important.

Trail Etiquette

Every now and then, while running down a trail enjoying the heck out of the day, you'll come across some sledders pulled over on the side of the trail. It's common courtesy to stop and see if they're okay. Experienced riders will give you a thumbs-up and that's good enough—they're just stopping to stretch their legs, or have a snack or drink of water, or snap a picture of the moose just off the trail. Still, if you're the one pulled over and something *is* wrong with your ride, you'll be glad the next guy along stopped to see what's up. The most important thing is to be aware of the rules of the road. With snowmobiling it's a basic principal: ride right. Almost all the trails in Maine are wide enough to accept two sleds passing side by side, and some are quite a bit wider. However, things can get dangerous in a hurry if you tend to use the whole trail up by riding in the middle. Think of it as driving a car (with no seatbelt or airbags). Always stay in your own lane. The closing speed of two sleds going toward each other on a trail is sometimes more than one hundred mph, much too fast for safe reaction times. Whenever I get a little throttle happy, I remind myself that you never know what's coming around the bend.

The other rule to trail riding is to let the oncoming riders know how many sleds they should expect to encounter. My first day of trail riding on the Yamaha I spent waving back at the oncoming sleds, thinking, *Gosh, everyone is so friendly*. As the day progressed, I noticed they weren't, in fact, waving at me but signaling to me the number of riders in their group. So, the first rider of a three-sled pack would hold up two fingers as he went by, meaning that I should expect two more riders behind him. The next rider would hold up one finger, and the last would hold up a closed fist, meaning he was the last in line.

I am *sure* Dan meant to tell me about this before we left that morning. I figured it out by afternoon that day and have done it ever since, and I now get a little peeved when I pass the few folks who don't know or don't bother. The only time you get a free pass is if you're wearing mittens. Ever try to guess how many fingers someone's holding up while they're wearing mittens? Just assume there are a few more sleds still to come.

Basic trail rules: Ride right, and let oncoming riders know how many sleds they should expect to encounter.

Gear and Clothing

When I first started riding, I thought I'd be using my old snowmaking mittens. These are massive suede affairs that extend halfway up your forearm and are mostly waterproof. They may be perfect for blowing snow on Sugarloaf, but I quickly realized gloves are more practical than mittens on a snowmobile. It's just a little easier to flip to your high beams from low, or to switch on your hand warmers. In fact, the first year I rode I had all skiing gear and an old modular helmet. It did the trick, I suppose, but I have slowly switched to gear that is made specifically for riding.

Having gear that is purpose-built is well worth it and I have managed to spread it out over a few years, alleviating a big upfront expenditure. Windproofing is as important as waterproofing and there are a dozen or so companies that make snowmobiling gear. With a little patience one can find some good deals, particularly in the spring when stores are clearing their shelves. Likewise with helmets. A half a dozen companies make helmets of various styles, ranging from chinless with just a plexi visor, modulars that open to various degrees, or open-faced BMX style helmets that require a pair of goggles. Many offer an electrical plug-in from the sled's wiring harness that heats and defrosts the helmet's face shield. Different folks like different helmets for different reasons. Besides the obvious safety factor, it is mostly just too cold to ride without one.

Trailers

Remember that old trailer out back of my in-laws' house, behind the woodpile? That is what they call a clamshell trailer, and to be honest it was a big pain in the butt. Clamshells are a single-axle trailer with a short tongue leading to the tow hitch. The trailer itself is consists of a deck and an aluminum cover that opens in a manner similar to a—wait for it—clamshell. You open the top, release a latch in the front, and the deck tilts down until it meets the ground. Then you can back a sled off or drive one on. During either of these maneuvers, at some point you will hit the tipping point of the tilting deck and the whole works slams down, or up, with the sled and rider hanging on, thinking something just broke. After you are loaded up, or unloaded and ready to ride, all you have to do is close the lid by lowering it into some incredibly narrow slots that are usually warped from use, or full of ice, or both.

Simple mechanical objects of this nature have always had a way of eluding me, and historically my patience is pretty thin when confronted with an obstinate device like this. Recognizing that my snowmobiling habit would likely mean the destruction of his trailer, Dan decided we should upgrade for the next winter. We traded up for a bigger, boxier rig that had a wonderful new feature. The whole back wall of the trailer was hinged in such a way that, when lowered, the rider had a gradual ramp leading in or out, making the transfer about a thousand times easier. You still had to back out, but there was ample head room, sort of, and it towed nicely behind the truck.

It's conceivable that we'd still have this rig even now, but we seem to be always adding sleds to our little fleet, and so most recently we upgraded to a new drive-through trailer, twenty feet long, with dual axles and inside storage cubbies. We can easily fit three snowmobiles inside with room to spare. The best feature is that there are door ramps on either end, making it a breeze to load and unload without having to back up or back out. You just drive in the back at the end of the day, and the next morning you can drive right out the front ramp, which opens to the starboard (passenger side for those of you who didn't grow up on a boat).

It's pretty slick, and the only downside I can see is that being so long it tends to catch the wind going up the road. It's unnerving to be hammering up Interstate 95 in a gale of wind and have the trailer start fishtailing from one lane to the next. Having two axles makes it a dream to back into tight spots, but in my experience it's a good idea never to drive into a place where you don't have an easy way to drive out.

Last but not least . . .

The second year I was riding I had only just started to accumulate some of these things. We had a new trailer, two sleds, and a motley assortment of gear that was doing the trick. That winter, 2014–2015,

If you can find a group of people who are honest, knowledgeable, and fun to talk with, like those I have found at my local sled shop, then those are folks you should do business with.

turned out to be one of the snowiest on record for the state of Maine. Everywhere we went, and even in Liberty, I was getting the old Viper stuck in amazingly deep snow. Being of the lake racer, trail performance variety, this snowmobile is extremely fast and handles well on hard-packed surfaces but is almost useless breaking trail in deep snow. Where we found groomed trails there was no problem, but getting to some out-of-the-way places that are rarely groomed, I started to run into a lot of problems. The truth is, I got stuck everywhere I went. Those who have ridden for years can tell you that a trail sled is great, *on* trails. *Off* trails, it can be problematic.

At the end of that season I vowed not to go riding again until I had a bigger sled, with deeper lugs (also called *paddles*) on the track. The Yamaha had a 121-inch track and small 1-inch lugs. I tried once to explain what a track was to a friend from Alabama and ended up comparing racing slicks on a racecar with studded snow tires on a plow truck. I was looking for something in the 140- to 150-inch range with at least 1.5-inch lugs and I didn't much care who the manufacturer was. The next fall, after a summer of research, I found what I was looking for. I now ride a Ski-Doo Renegade Backcountry, and I am thrilled with it. This particular sled is a crossover, meaning it's a hybrid between trail riding and off-trail riding. Sporting a 146-inch track with 1.6-inch lugs, this snowmobile is equally at home riding the unplowed logging roads of the Allagash and the smooth flat trails of the Moosehead region. It's great around the local trails in

Liberty and is up to the task of breaking the trail down onto the lake. The Backcountry won't win any speed contests and that's fine by me. I'm content to top out around eighty mph, though I rarely do so.

By no means do I mean to suggest one brand over the other, here. Each of the four snowmobile manufacturers has a model similar to my sled and they are all as capable. Yamaha makes a BTX and XTX, Polaris has its RMK line, and Arctic Cat makes the Crossfire. What it came down to for me was the shop that sold me my machine. If you can find a group of people that are honest, knowledgeable, and fun to talk with, like those I have found at my local sled shop, then those are folks you should do business with. The favorite subject for snowmobilers is, of course, snowmobiles, and there are plenty of folks who are the definition of brand loyalty. I know people who have only ever ridden Cats and absolutely swear by them. Same thing with Yamaha. Same thing with Polaris. In the end, everyone finds what suits them best, and as long as you're out having fun on the snow, that's all that matters.

Sugarloaf

Oquossoc • Rangeley

Rangeley
Lake

Farmington

The Western
Mountains

3
The Western Mountains

In my opinion, snowmobiling in Maine is broken down into four distinct geographic areas. The County, meaning Aroostook, is the largest county in Maine and qualifies as its own unique destination. Second, coming south just slightly is the greater Jackman area and the Moosehead Lake region. I've lumped the Baxter State Park region in here, though of course the clubs near Katahdin, from Millinocket up to Libby Camps outside of Ashland, could make a compelling argument for their own area. Next is Eastern Maine—the whole of Washington and Hancock Counties, and a chunk of Waldo and Penobscot—generally, everything east of Interstate 95. Lastly, the Rangeley Lakes region, including Farmington and Sugarloaf, is basically synonymous with the Western Mountains.

It's also true that there is a spider web of local trails through all of Midcoast and Southern Maine. Some of my favorite rides have been on the local trails that may never see a groomer, and there are many riders who never stray farther afield than their backyard. One thing to keep in mind with these more southern areas is that the weather isn't as cold as "up north" and so streams, ponds, and lakes are often not safe to cross. If there isn't a local club marking trails, you'd better have a good info system set up with the locals.

The Western Mountains cover of nearly one hundred miles of rivers, lakes, mountains, and valleys. This includes a large chunk of the Appalachian Trail, parts of three counties, and the state's big ski resorts, Sunday River in Bethel, Saddleback in Rangeley, and Sugarloaf in Carrabassett Valley. Starting on the southern end of Somerset County through all of Franklin and finishing with the northern part of Oxford County, the Western Mountains routinely get crushed with big snows. Early in the winter the mountains are the beneficiaries of "upslope" snow. This happens when moisture is rolling along to the east, minding its own business, but then slams into the mountains, gets pushed up and cools as it does, forms clouds, and, if there's enough energy, results in snow. Weather radar doesn't always pick up these small snowstorms.

Ask a local for an updated snow report because just twenty miles toward the coast the weather will be sunny and warm while it's dumping in the mountains.

It's nice to know someone in the area for an updated snow report because just twenty miles toward the coast the weather will be sunny and warm while it's dumping along the Canadian border. Very often the area north of Rangeley Lake, starting in the small village of Oquossoc, is the first part of the state to get rideable snow. The Park and Ride in Oquossoc around December 15 is routinely full of trailers belonging to hard-core snow chasers. My first two trips of the 2016–2017 season were in this area, before Christmas, and I was pleased to be riding untracked powder on the logging roads that veer off from the ITS.

My very first snowmobile trip in the Western Mountains, not counting the shoveling trip when I was snowmaking, started in

Carrabassett Valley, where we were borrowing an A-frame cottage from some family friends. Mary and I had driven up early in the afternoon, just ahead of a small snowstorm, and Dan and Carol were coming behind us with the old clamshell trailer and sleds. Being the first trip anywhere in about ten years, and likely because the roads were a sloppy, snowy mess, the trailer decided to blow all the bearings out of the left side tire. Dan and Carol got to spend the afternoon on the side of Route 3 fixing it. By the time they showed up in the valley, well after dark, I was chafing at the delay in riding (*I mean, just put a new tire on and go, right?*) and Dan had remembered half the reasons he got out of the sport.

The next morning, we followed the bumpy connector trail to Sugarloaf Regional Airport, a tiny town-owned airport along the Carrabassett River, and there got onto the ITS. We were on the Arnold Trail Club system, and I quickly discovered the joys of riding on a groomed trail. This was, in fact, my first experience with the ITS and also the day when I thought everyone was waving to me. We rode to Stratton and back that day, and the views of the Bigelow Range and Flagstaff Lake were outstanding. I had often admired the steep, stretched-out peaks of the Bigelows from the ski trails of Sugarloaf just across the valley. I was seeing those same mountains from a new angle as we rolled around the hills just underneath them, and it was exhilarating.

This was my first day using a local trail map, and I found it appealed greatly to my sense of direction and navigation. I already felt a little bit at home due to my two years working on Sugarloaf, so that probably helped as well. I spent a little time by myself that trip looking for trail access to the mountain, knowing full well that riding a sled on Sugarloaf was off-limits. I had remembered a night making snow on the lower east side of the mountain, next to all the condos.

Danno, along with another fellow, who for some reason was nicknamed the Guv'nor, and I had just finished shutting down the snowguns and had cleaned up all the hoses when we saw the lights from three snowmobiles leave a parking lot and roar up the trail. Being fiercely protective of his mountain (and almost certainly thrilled at the prospect of a high-speed chase), Danno yelled for us to hop on our sleds and "go get 'em," which of course we did without further prodding. We caught up to them and I remember it being like a Wild West shootout. We circled them as viciously as we could a couple of times and when they were corralled, he gave them a good talking to. The three of us escorted them back to their condo like we were Patton's Third Army. Since then I have yet to find a way onto the mountain, short of the numerous parking lots, but I haven't totally given up either.

A month later we were back with the island school kids (at the time, Mary was the schoolteacher on Monhegan, in one of the last one-room schools in the state) and I had convinced one of the fathers, a fellow lobsterman named Lucas, to rent a sled in Stratton and ride with me for a day while everyone else skied. I had a plan to ride over to Rangeley Lake and back, and that is just what we did. By this time, after nearly two months of riding my Yamaha, I was feeling like a seasoned pro. With Lucas looking more or less comfortable on his snowmobile from Flagstaff Rentals in Stratton, I tore off out of town and headed west for the thirty-mile trip through the mountains.

Normally when riding in a group the lead rider waits for everyone to catch up at each trail junction, or stop sign, or road crossing. A mile out of town I stopped and waited for Lucas. And waited. And waited. Just as I decided to turn around and go see what was up, I saw him puttering around the last corner. We crossed the road and off I went, loving the acceleration on the flat, wide trails. Five miles later I stopped and waited at the next junction. And waited. And waited. He showed up just as I had turned around and was headed back to see if he was broken down or stuck in a snowbank. Half an hour later the situation

Normally when riding in a group the lead rider waits for everyone to catch up at each trail junction, or stop sign, or road crossing.

repeated itself and even I could see the pattern developing. Lucas had decided he was quite comfortable plugging along about twenty-five mph, and I would just have to wait. Lobstermen in Maine are known primarily for several characteristics, among them healthy doses of stubbornness and impatience, and between the two of us we were exemplifying each.

We ended up in Oquossoc, across the lake from Rangeley, and found an old diner that was serving food. We thumped in, hung our helmets and jackets by the roaring wood-stove, and settled down at the bar for a burger. I've found that nearly every place that caters to riders will have a spot by the heat for hanging gear to dry. It's polite, however, to stomp off as much snow as you can outside. After lunch in Oquossoc and a nifty straight shot down the length of Rangeley Lake (where Lucas may have seen forty mph), we settled in for the ride back to Stratton, marveling at, among other things, some of the huge maple sugaring operations. Overall the day had been a great run, and a fun chance to scout the area for later trips.

The next winter I only rode the area for one stretch, in March. We were planning a family trip, so I Googled "cabins in Rangeley" and picked the one that seemed to have something for everyone. We planned to be there for most of a week and we had skis, snowshoes, snowmobiles—basically every bit of winter sports equipment we owned. Mary and Dan would bring the trailer with his sled, but I had decided that it would be a fun thing to ride my snowmobile the whole way north from Liberty. I asked Dan to drop me off down the road from his house, at Frye Mountain in Montville. This was the start of the ITS in the area, so I knew it would be recently groomed.

Almost two hundred miles later I drove into the driveway of the cabin on the eastern shore of Rangeley Lake. I had a wonderful time plotting my route, making sure I had gas and, of course, lunch, and was pleased that I only took one wrong turn, right off the bat in Unity. It was the longest run I had done on the Viper. As the crow flies, the mileage is something like eighty-five miles, but of course you can't go directly. From Unity up to Newport, then west to Skowhegan, Anson, and Strong, and then the last push along the Sandy River and over the mountains, it's a superb trip and very well marked. I loved the thought of this trip, and the planning that went with it and having a purpose and destination. I didn't realize that this would become my mantra for snowmobiling, but it certainly sparked the fire.

The rest of the week we spent alternately skiing and riding snowmobiles. Dan and I got in a ride to the New Hampshire border and back, with a stop at Bosebuck Mountain Camps for lunch. The Bosebuck Camps are located in the extreme west side of Maine on

Aziscohos Lake and are a classic example of Maine's sporting camps. Catering to hunters and fishermen, and snowmobilers in winter, they are a remote sanctuary for cold and hungry riders. I've always had a penchant for these kinds of backwoods buildings, tucked under a ridge on the north side of some lake, complete with mounted heads of deer, moose, bobcat, and the like in the main lodge. The cabins are often rustic in appearance and accommodations compared to downstate establishments, but when you come in from fifty miles of five-degree riding, it feels just as good as any posh Portland hotel.

Unfortunately, the winter of 2015–2016 was a terrible snow year for New England and in particular for Maine. I should have anticipated this lack of snow because I had just purchased that new Backcountry. There was almost no rideable snow until the end of January, and what the state got then was quickly gone. That winter was the only year I hadn't ridden in the Western Mountains, so by the fall of 2016 I was hoping to make up for it.

The first ride of the year we planned as a day trip from the Park and Ride in Oquossoc. We were to meet up with a work friend of Dan's and go ride the border cut, between Maine and Canada. We missed it. A massive Arctic front dropped out of Hudson Bay, complete with gale force winds, and it was simply too rough on the ocean for me to get off the island. This happens frequently during Maine's winters. It's not enough to have a nor'easter with all the big wind and big seas one produces. No, after many winter storms spin their way off to the east, Mother Nature likes to let all that wind swing into the northwest and scream down to and out over the Gulf of

Maine. It is all too common for the island to endure four or five days of storm force winds. You get used to it, learn to love it or at least tolerate it. Or you move somewhere that's not all about the wind for seven months a year. But Jarrod, Dan's old riding pal, had set the hook pretty well. I had heard several times the story of these guys riding the border cut, very early in the season (as early as Thanksgiving some years) and of the huge, steep hills that were common there.

I was in touch with Jarrod later that week and naturally he reported that the riding had been great. Untracked powder, cold and sunny, and a handful of moose sheds. (It's common, early in the winter, to be riding along a trail and see half a set of antlers sitting in the snow where they have fallen off the moose after the fall rut. Well, maybe not common, but it does happen, I'm told. I've never been lucky enough to come across one.)

Finally, the wind let go, the ocean crossing seemed manageable, and I was soon on the phone booking a cabin with Bald Mountain Camps and on my way. This time I had lugged another lobsterman along, Eben, who had just bought himself an older Polaris RMK. This sled is arguably the first in the line of sleds known as mountain sleds—indeed, RMK stands for Rocky Mountain King. They're very capable off-trail sleds, but Eben's was throwing a little smoke and he wanted it looked at. Turns out that little bit of smoke had a touch of antifreeze in it, and that turned into a rebuild of more than half the engine. Luckily, we had the old Renegade in the trailer as a spare so we dropped his off across the street from the Park and Ride at Oquossoc Marine and were soon gearing up. Remember when I said this was my first ride of the year? Forgot my boots. Back across the street to buy a new pair and then we were off.

I was going on some half-vague directions from Jarrod and trying out my new GPS at the same time. There was almost no one on the trails and they had been groomed from the new snow a few nights prior, making for great early season trail riding. About fifteen miles northwest of town, we took the first turn off of the ITS and followed some old tracks. We didn't necessarily know where we were, but it didn't really matter. With full tanks of gas, confident we could back-track along our own tracks, we ripped farther into the wilderness. If this sounds sketchy, it's not. Riders all over the state do this every day of every season.

Every now and then we'd come around a corner and see a cut-ting off to the side where people had veered off to blast up a hill. As the miles wore on the tracks became fewer and the trail grew more narrow until it seemed to end in a small clearing along the top of a ridge. Seemed to, but didn't. One single sled trail kept on through the opening and, still kind of searching for this mythical border cut, we went right along with it. It turned into a single-lane goat path going down about a mile or so, and it came out finally on a logging road. It had been kind of a neat little trip coming down the side of the mountain, but honestly, I probably wouldn't have done it had there not already been someone to break it out ahead of me.

Now on the logging road, we could go right or left, and we chose right, went about a mile, found the road ended in woods and then a gate, which we went around, and we popped out at a crossroads on the international border!

Eben pulled up next to me and we took a couple of pictures of a sign saying to check in to Coburn Gore for inspection, which we felt didn't apply to us. I noticed a Customs-managed game camera pointed at us. We weren't doing anything wrong, but I liked that it was there. Someone is always watching! (I can hear it now: two young lobstermen snowmobiling off trail and *not* doing anything wrong? Yah, sure.) We took a right and wound our way along the border, avoiding the three-foot stone monuments that mark the delineation between the United States and Canada. Soon we reached a massive pine blown across the trail that hadn't been cleaned up enough for us to pass so we turned around and went the other way. I was still looking for that big hill I'd heard so much about and I was about to find it.

We went back past the game camera, took the left, and maneuvered around another big pine and suddenly there we were at the bottom of a big, big hill. We shut the sleds off and craned our necks up, looking at some impossibly deep water bars in the first half of the pitch and two sled tracks that were laid down on it. The big question was, did that guy come down the hill or go up it?

An hour later we had our answer. Neither of us got farther than halfway up. Those big water bars—deep trenches cut across mountains to prevent erosion by promoting water runoff—robbed all the momentum we had. Many mountains in Maine have these water bars, and not just the ski mountains. They are often three or four feet deep, so not something you want to hit at speed. After the bars, it was just too steep for the tracks to get a good purchase and we were forced to turn around, which on a steep hill is no easy task. The rest of the day was spent exploring the logging and hunting camp roads, and we pulled into Bald Mountain Camps that night ready for a beer.

Less than a week later I was back, with Dan and Jeff this time, and we were there to get to the top of that hill or die trying. We got closer, but the carnage was worse the second time around. Six inches of fresh snow brought the total coverage to somewhere around three feet. Dan was the first to go up and had the same problem with

Just above my handlebars you can see our tracks coming from the goat path. You can also see the mountain bar.

water bars that Eben and I had experienced. I was next, and when I went by Dan he was looking at his new Polaris trail sled upside down in a pile of snow, steam wafting out of the cowling.

This time I was ready for the dips. I kept my momentum through the middle of the hill, charging upward all the time, standing up and shifting my weight to counter the twists of the hill, the top getting closer all the time. To keep from flying off the snowmobile and to help the balance of the sled itself, I was using the mountain bar. This is a semi-rigid handle in the middle of the handlebars. At this point I was forced to roll the sled hard left. Unfortunately, I had to let go of the throttle to grab the mountain bar. The machine instantly slowed and I knew I had lost any chance of seeing the top. The sled veered back to the right and, though I was able to get a hand back on the throttle, it spun itself deeper into the snow, losing momentum and purchase. The hill and deep snow had won another round.

For a split second my mind was blank, and then the sled started creeping to the right, and downhill. Realizing I had to do something fast to keep the sled from taking a catastrophic five-hundred-yard roll, I jumped off and planted my feet just below the snowmobile and brought the whole rig to a rest on my shoulder.

The sled settled a bit into the snow and I was able to relax slightly, look downhill, and give a thumbs-up to Jeff and Dan. By this time Jeff had arrived at Dan's sled and they had succeeded in rolling it back upright. They saw me motion to them that I'd need help, hung their heads, and started slogging up through the drifts toward me. It's a tricky business to roll a six-hundred-pound chunk of plastic and steel on flat ground. On this hill, it was going to take all three of us to avoid losing control of it. After some discussion of the relative effects of gravity on small machines, we got the Backcountry turned around and, thinking the worst was over, off I went down the hill.

The second I let go of the brake, the sled rocketed forward. Most folks would have considered this beforehand, but, in my defense,

As many riders will tell you, pictures don't do justice to the steepness of the hill. Photo by Jeffrey Johnston.

there wasn't any other option *but* going straight down. In the time it took to get to the other two sleds, I was holding the brake as hard as I could, the track was locked up, and I was skidding at twenty-five mph, basically out of control, bouncing into and out of the water bars. I shot by Dan and Jeff's rides as the hill became less steep. Finally, I gained some semblance of control.

We all met again back at the tree with the game camera and discussed the entire event. Jeff said that after watching Dan and me get creamed, he had decided not to bother with it and in fact he was the only one who didn't roll his sled over. Most people would've just watched us struggle from a comfortable spot at the bottom, but Jeff isn't wired that way. He slogged up that hill, through all that snow, to help both of us out. I'm sure he had a few choice words for us under his breath, but he did it and we were glad of it.

We spent that afternoon on the logging roads in the far western reaches of Maine. We had my GPS and a *Gazetteer* and we rode as far as we could, taking whatever snow-covered road looked interesting. Parmanchee, Magalloway, and other names I had never seen were popping up on various signs. Every now and then we'd come around a corner to find a set of hunting camps lined up in a row, or a four corners where it seemed no one had been since fall.

A ride like this is one of the truly great things about snowmobiling in Maine. There is always something cool to look at. Often, it'll get me to thinking, as we go off down the trail, about the person who was inclined to build himself a camp out in the willy-wacks and what things were like here sixty years ago. There may be no way to know the fella who built his hideout, but one thing is sure: Not much changes way back in the woods. That's why I like it so much.

Recommended Ride

I always remind myself that the trails around Rangeley Lake—ITS 84 and 89 as well as the numerous local club trails—offer up some of the most stunning views from any snowmobile trail in Maine. If you were to wake up and find yourself in the middle of Rangeley Lake on your snowmobile, besides being generally extremely lucky, you'd be able to ride in any direction and find one of at least seven trails heading from water's edge to Rangeley, Oquossoc, a dozen of the local mountains, several large maple sugar operations, numerous sporting camps, New Hampshire, Saddleback Mountain ski resort, and miles of unnamed logging roads. These trails are impeccably kept, and you'll be wishing you had your camera if you go up the spur of East Kennebago Mountain.

If you're looking to get out of the house at the end of January, check out the annual Rangeley Snodeo. This four-day winter carnival includes live auctions and casino nights, fireworks, a snowmobile parade that often draws many hundreds of sleds, and several classes of racing for pros and amateurs alike. Maybe the biggest draw is the Rave-X Show, a high-flying group of riders who specialize in tricks and big jumps (like motocross but on snowmobiles). These stunt riders elicit many *oohs* and *aahs* from the crowds as they fly fifty or sixty feet through the air, taking off from massive snow ramps plowed up by the clubs' groomers.

Katahdin and
Moosehead
Region

Baxter
State Park

Pittston
Farm

Millinocket

Moosehead
Lake

Jackman

4

Katahdin and Moosehead Region

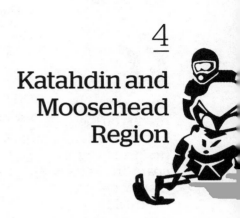

The state of Maine has a lot of roads, and Mainers, some of us, are apt to hop in the old truck and go for a ride on a day off. Mainers carry different things with them on a ride: fishing poles, cameras, hunting rifles, or in my case, sometimes half a rack of ribs (Mary is still disgusted with me about that moose-scouting excursion—we never saw a moose but I had a wonderful lunch on a bridge overlooking the bog by Little Spencer).

Everyone is aware of Interstate 95, the biggest road in Maine. No doubt it's a handy little highway for getting to the far reaches of the state or getting out of the state altogether in mud season. However, there are numerous byways that have acquired greater or lesser amounts of notoriety over the years. Certainly, the most famous dirt road in Maine is the Golden Road, running from the Canadian border north of Jackman across to Millinocket.

A close second might be the Stud Mill Road, on which my friends and I spent some time, in high school, trying to shoot birds. In Liberty, they have the Mary Ordway Road, a favorite among the mushroom and deer hunters. The vast majority of these dirt roads are the domain of logging trucks. Indeed, these roads are often built and maintained, including grading in the summer and plowing in

> The key to driving on these back roads, besides having a spare tire, water, map, compass, overnight survival gear, food, and a cell phone, is remembering to pull over when encountering two things: moose and logging trucks.

the winter, by the logging companies. They crisscross both public and private land and are generally open access. The key to driving on these roads, besides having a spare tire, water, map, compass, overnight survival gear, food, and a cell phone, is remembering to pull over when encountering two things: moose and logging trucks. They both have the right of way. In the fall, a large bull moose might just view your vehicle as a rival bull and attempt to engage in battle with your front bumper.

At the same time, it's wise to remember that truck drivers get paid purely on the amount of wood they haul out of the deep woods, not by the hour, so it behooves them to drive quickly from the log yard in the woods to the mill in town. When you encounter one of these massive machines on say, the Rocky Brook Road, it will be going fast and is not inclined, or able, to slow down and let your S-10 pick its way through the latest potholes. The accepted behavior is to pull over and let it pass, and then continue on in five minutes when the dust or snow has settled from its passing.

Dusty, poorly marked back roads notwithstanding, there are just as many main roads that have gained attention for various reasons. Almost any main road in the state will sooner rather than later provide you with a trip through mountains and valleys, streams and rivers, classic diners and watering holes, mill towns and long stretches of woods, and any number of the oddities so often found along Maine roads.

My favorite is Route 201. Most of us don't know where 201 starts, but everyone with a snowmobile knows where it ends: Jackman. Route 201 actually starts in Topsham and runs parallel with Interstate 95, quickly joining the Kennebec River and following it through Waterville and then Fairfield. Here the interstate goes on its way north to Bangor, but 201 keeps with the Kennebec and turns to the northwest, running through Skowhegan, Solon, and Bingham until it arrives at The Forks. This is where the Dead River, from Flagstaff Lake, meets the Kennebec River, coming from Moosehead Lake, and it is a very popular spot for whitewater rafting in Maine. It is also in the heart of snow country. From The Forks, 201 continues on some thirty miles into the higher mountains of the region. The road becomes more winding with houses every half mile or so with nothing but woods in between. You'd better have filled your gas tank up earlier because you won't have a chance until, finally, 201 comes up over the last ridge with a view of spectacular Attean Pond and drops you into the frontier town of Jackman.

Jackman is a top destination for many snowmobilers. You owe it to yourself to ride here at least once. Once you ride it, you'll want to come back for more. It's the only area that I've been to every year since I started riding. The town labels itself as the Switzerland of Maine, often getting early season snow, but just as importantly, there's late season snow too. Riding out of Jackman can be done as late as mid-April some years, when the snow is long gone everywhere else. The town itself is geared purely for snowmobilers—the in-town trails are full of turn-offs for lodges, fuel, restaurants, and repair shops.

My first trip to ride snowmobiles in Jackman was midway through the first year I was riding, and that was also my first trip up Route 201. We left Liberty, four of us in Dan's truck (Dan, Jeff, Kole, also from the island, and me) towing the clamshell with the two old sleds and planning to rent two more rides when we got there. I had found a set of cabins for rent just a couple of miles north of Jackman, in Dennistown. Conveniently the owner of Spruce Meadow Cabins also owned the local rental sled business, Bald Mountain Rentals (not the same Bald Mountain as the one in Oquossoc). Cresting that last mountain before coming into town, we slowed and took in the view.

Below us lay frozen Attean Pond with its numerous coves and small islands. Beyond that lay the last few wooded miles of Maine, and then Canada in the distance, distinguishable by a ridge of windmills swinging slowly and steadily. If you haven't seen this, it is spectacular on a clear day. We went on down for a mile or so into town, and here is where you start to understand: In the winter, Jackman is a mecca for snowmobilers.

There were sleds everywhere. Hotels, stores, diners, and gas stations on either side of the street had more snowmobiles in the parking lots than anything else. Pickup trucks either with trailers or sled decks in their beds were everywhere. The road signs in town were as much for riders as they were for vehicles, with the telltale black arrows on yellow signboards. In fact, three different ITS trails run by or into the town, as well as a plethora of local trails leading to various sporting camps, repair shops, lakes, and the Border Riders' club house. The Border Riders snowmobile club is possibly the most well-known in the state. They take their trail maintenance seriously and it shows. Our cabin was right on Route 201 but also on the end of a small connector trail kept groomed by the owner of the cabins and used solely by his guests.

The next morning, we were on our way. We were armed with a motley assortment of gear, a trail map, my Viper, Dan's Renegade, and the two rentals, which were newer Ski-Doos. Never having ridden the area, we had no set agenda or destination, and that is often the best way to head out for a ride. We rode the first day toward Pittston Farm, a former logging compound thirty miles northeast of Jackman. The Farm, as it's affectionately called by everyone in the area, is a hub of activity in winter, often fueling and serving food to more than five hundred riders on any given day. The owners, Guy and Jennifer Mills, run the operation year-round, and that includes grooming nearly one hundred miles of trails. I often think of The Farm during those crushing nor'easters, as its remoteness rivals Monhegan's in many ways, and I like the thought of them shrugging off the bad weather and going on about their business.

At one point, Dan informed us we were headed down a part of Route 66 called Burn Down Alley. This is a long straightaway that is famous for riders opening up the throttle on their engines, sometimes with catastrophic results. We didn't burn down any of our rides that day, but it wasn't for lack of trying.

The next day we went north again but this time continued on around the top of Moosehead Lake and managed to, all of a sudden, turn a corner on a trail that dropped us directly under Mount Kineo. I'd like to say I planned it, as I was generally in charge of navigation, but the truth is my education in the geography of Maine and its snowmobile trails had only just begun. I had no idea we'd end up here and just got lucky. I played it as coolly as I could, never missing a beat as we roared up to the foot of the seven-hundred-foot-high cliff and stopped to check it out.

If you haven't seen Kineo, it's a truly impressive mountain surrounded on three sides by the biggest lake in Maine. Standing 1,800 feet tall, Kineo is a distinct landmark fifty miles in any direction. Three years later, Mary and I hiked it in the fall. The views were well worth it, although the main trail is not for the faint of heart—one is often inches away from the edge of the cliff and there are no handrails. I have heard that in the winter the game wardens will set up an observation station at the top to keep an eye on ice fishermen (which seems like a lot of trouble, if you ask me).

Heading back to Jackman after a rather large lunch (a meal at The Birches Resort on Moosehead Lake is a can't-miss), I was content to ride at the back of the pack. At one point we stopped at one of the ITS crossroads and after a lot of discussion, we went toward what they determined was the way home. I trusted them explicitly until we started seeing signs indicating Pittston Farm was getting closer and Jackman was getting farther away. At that point, realizing we were well off course and after a lot of "nice job, numbnuts" and "you couldn't drive your way out of a wet paper bag," we fueled up at The Farm. It was decided that Kole wasn't needed on point and I would resume the lead. Luckily, we were there to ride, it was a nice day to add forty miles to the trip and, let's be honest, getting turned around is easy to do and all part of the fun.

Early the next March I was back at the same cabins and had again dragged Lucas along with me. This time I would ride Dan's Renegade and Lucas would be on the Viper, which I informed him was entirely capable of going faster than his rental sled from Stratton. We left the first morning at eight or so. It was three degrees and windy after the previous night's light snow. This was, in fact, the same day we'd find ourselves in the ground blizzard on Moosehead Lake, but that wasn't the only trouble we ran into that day.

The first issue that day was a problem just for me. One of the things that no one ever really mentions about riding a snowmobile all day is dealing with certain calls of nature. Now, going number one is no problem, for a guy at least, as you just pull your sled over and let fly into the woods, preferably downwind. This particular day, however, breakfast, or the last night's dinner, was not agreeing with me. Knowing this, I had armed myself with several folded-up paper towels before we left the cabin, stashed in various pockets. Ten miles out of town, once again headed for Pittston Farm, I motioned Lucas to go on ahead as I had business to attend to. Luckily, I had those paper towels. I soon caught up with him at the next stop sign and off we went, enjoying the lack of company on the trails, but I soon realized something still wasn't right in my stomach. I motioned him to go on ahead, which he did, laughing. By this time, I knew something was up and I was probably not done with my trailside stops and was just hoping I could hold on for the last five miles, mainly because my supply of paper towels was used up.

I didn't make it. My dilemma had reached maximum proportions. I was out of paper towels, deep in the Maine woods in the dead of winter, no leaves handy, and I wasn't about to use a handful of cold powdery snow. Out came the pocketknife. I figured the entire front of my T-shirt would be sufficient, and also maybe the only article of clothing I could spare that wouldn't leave me freezing any more than I already was. After cutting a large square hole from the shirt to function as a hygiene product, I was able to move on. Fortunately, that was the end of my problems for the day, at least as

> **Every summer, the trails get grown in with brush, the countless small wooden bridges need attention, and rerouting of trails is planned and then executed. This work—and it's a lot of work —is all done by volunteers.**

far as bodily functions went. In hindsight, I suppose I should just be happy it didn't happen on the wide expanses of the lake.

That night when we got back to the cabin, an old buddy of ours met us for some beers and we got to telling stories. Lucas was still chortling at my adventures of the morning and that got Greg going on the time one of his buddies had the same problem but wasn't lucky enough to have started out with any paper products whatsoever. Sure enough, turns out this fella used the same knife-to-the-shirt trick that I had mastered just that morning, and when he was done telling us, I stood up, pulled off my sweatshirt and said, "Did it look like this?!"

My shirt was intact except for a square directly over my stomach, the edge of the cut ragged in my haste that morning. We all got a good laugh out of it and I'm sure plenty of other riders have done exactly the same thing. I often wish I had kept that shirt for the sole purpose of seeing Mary's puzzled expression as she went to fold it while doing laundry.

The Millinocket area was the first place I took the new Backcountry for an overnight, and I loved it. In December 2015, Maine had received several small storms and barely any cold weather. I was itching to go for a real ride, but all I was seeing on social media was that clubs weren't grooming yet and most were just starting on the essential job of trail work. Every summer, the trails get grown in with brush, the countless small wooden bridges need attention, and rerouting of trails is planned and then executed. This work—and it's a lot of work—is all done by volunteers. Every club has a handful of devotees that put in their time to complete all these projects. With Christmas just around the corner and more snow likely, they were rushing to get it all done, and many clubs were putting out the call for help.

I discussed it with Dan and we decided to meet up with the JoMary Riders crew at their clubhouse for a day of chainsaw work. The JoMary Riders club takes its name from the same lakes, and it may well be the luckiest snowmobile club in Maine. Their trails offer spectacular views of Mount Katahdin, the state's tallest mountain as well as the northern end of the Appalachian Trail. We were late getting there, having forgotten a pair of riding boots, and by the time we were ready to go no one was around. They had work to do and weren't inclined to wait on a couple of yahoos no one had ever heard of, and I don't blame them. Finally, after wandering around the local connector trail looking for signs to the Parkway (whatever that was), we met a local gentleman who was thinking of going for a ride himself and would be happy to show us the way. After a tour of his magnificent house on the edge of South Twin Lake, we followed him out of town and soon were hot on the tails of the work crew. They were brushing out a trail named "The 109" and had been at it for some time. Every hundred feet or so there were signs of blow downs and leaners (helmet-slappers) that had been cut and thrown off to the side of the trail. When we finally rounded a corner and found them, three sleds of various ages and conditions with the owners, also of varied ages and conditions, they took a break for a minute.

"You must be Matt Weber?"

"Yes. Sorry we're late. Looks like fun."

"Come all the way from Monhegan to help do this?"

"Yep. Too rough to haul traps."

"Good. Got a Husqvarna, I see. I run Stihls myself."

"Well, as long as they start, right?"

It was a stupid thing to say. Dan keeps his chainsaws, all five of them, in tip-top shape. (Don't ask why one person needs five chainsaws. I once pointed out to him that he only has two arms but five saws and he glared at me, clearly wondering why his oldest daughter had married such a complete imbecile.) The chains are all good, fluids topped off, carbs clean, and they *always* start.

Not this day, though. I hopped off my sled and grabbed the saw off the back, popped the choke, and gave the pull cord a rip. And then another rip. I pulled twenty times and that foolish saw wouldn't go. The club guys had already turned their backs on me ("that's why I run a Stihl, right there") and Dan laughed as he left me to figure it out and started chucking logs off the side of the trail. It finally went, after I had knocked my helmet into the snow and managed to rip the seat of my new sled with the chain. I turned up the trail with an air of victory, only to find it all cut and cleaned up, the crew heading around the next corner.

In truth, we were able to help some and I think they were glad we showed up, if for nothing more than the company, or the entertainment. They had been at it all day at this point and when, an hour or so later, the trail came to a T that had already been cleared, they thanked us. We all chatted for a few minutes and it became clear that they were responsible for keeping the better part of one hundred miles of trails up to snuff. Their parting shot of advice was to try the state park trail around Katahdin, and the next morning we did just that.

We trailered the sleds from Millinocket to the south entrance of Baxter State Park, the gatehouse at Togue Pond, and found we could go a little farther in to Abol Pond. I remembered a natural rock water slide we used to visit here as kids, and although we never climbed Katahdin, many do each summer. It's serious business, climbing here, and the most famous pitch, the nerve-racking Knife's Edge, may be the scariest section of hiking in New England. We parked the truck and trailer just after eight, but there were already some early-season fanatics in the parking lot and we didn't waste any time getting going. The trail around Katahdin is known as the Park Tote Road. I don't know what happens on it in the summer, but in the winter, it is a multiuse trail. We, of course, did not know this and halfway around the mountain, I was surprised to come upon a group of cross-country skiers hauling sleds full of winter camping gear.

Judging by the tracks in the fresh snow, we were the fourth and fifth sleds to take the tote road that day. It's a long haul all the way around the west side of Maine's biggest mountain, and a gorgeous one too. The thirty-odd mile route offers up views of Katahdin and also travels for a while along the Nesowadnehunk Stream as it passes under Doubletop Mountain. Eventually it brings you out by the Matagamon Gatehouse at the beginning of the Penobscot River's East Branch. It's a spectacular ride and fun to see the rangers' cabins and park signs along the trail, but there is one caveat. Since it's part of Baxter State Park, which is managed as a wildlife sanctuary and wilderness area, they don't allow it to be groomed, so it's not a ride for beginners, although a rider with a decent sense of direction and a capable sled would be likely to pull it off. We were lucky enough to arrive after a fresh snow-fall and had a relatively smooth ride. However, it wouldn't take much sled traffic to "bump up" the trail with moguls and that would turn an

The Park Tote Road is a spectacular ride. Since it's part of Baxter State Park, which is managed as a wildlife sanctuary and wilderness area, they don't allow it to be groomed, so it's not a ride for beginners. Also keep in mind that it is a multiuse trail.

otherwise pleasurable ride into a bone-jarring nightmare.

Once through the gate at Matagamon, we were pleased to find ourselves back on flat groomed trails. It was a shade early for lunch, even though the Matagamon general store looked tempting. These perfectly groomed trails led us directly in to Bowlin Camps about an hour later, the first sleds of the day for them. We fueled up and I marveled at the beauty of the spot. The owner chatted with us while we had lunch, discussing life along the upper reaches of the Penobscot River and land access issues that plague certain areas of the state. I poked around a few of the cabins thinking of future overnight trips and promised myself I'd be back someday. We left Bowlin headed on a beeline back to Abol, the truck, and the trailer, and were back in Liberty two hours later. Like so many of our trips, the planned part didn't go exactly as we thought, and yet it had been another unforgettable trip north.

I should mention that for a while I had been carrying the ashes of an old Walker hound under the backseat of my truck. His name was Tarzan; he was seven years old when I got him and suffering from post-traumatic stress disorder after years of coyote hunting. When Tarzan finally lost his nerve, the hunter, as I was told, announced his intention to take him out back and shoot him. This didn't sit well with the hunter's wife, who had developed a fondness for the stubborn jackass of a dog (he had a way, let me tell you) and so it was decided to bring him to the local humane society and see if some poor sot could be convinced to take him off to retire in the countryside. Maybe somewhere warm, and preferably with lots of couches.

What that dog ended up with was a full seven more years of island life with me and, eventually, Mary and her dog. The fall I acquired Tarzan, I had just returned from a summer of fishing for herring on George's Bank. I had already dated most of the single women on the island and had no current companion, so naturally it seemed like the right time to get a dog. Anyway, Tarzan had a new home and he took to it with vigor, or at least a willingness to nap on the furniture. One of the unique things about him was that he was born with only three toes on his front left foot, a fact that I noticed when I first saw him in the kennel. I thought he should start off on the island with a bit of mystique and so I concocted a story about him being in a savage one-on-one fight with a female black bear guarding her cubs. He played along wonderfully as he did have scars from his coyote days and it wasn't much of a leap for him to look like the old and grizzled veteran that he was. This story did a lot to impress the residents of the island, and I was heartened to hear, three years later, that several islanders not only still believed the story but also perpetuated it.

Tarzan became a large part of our lives, as most pets do, and when it was time to put him down, we did so sadly and with little fanfare knowing that's the way he would've wanted it. He did well by us, and we by him. When it was all over, the vet asked me if I'd like the ashes and I said yes without really thinking about it.

A view of Katahdin looking from Chesuncook Lake.

The small wooden box sat under the backseat of the truck for more than a year and then moved to the back of a newer truck. After more time passed, I realized I should bring him for a snowmobile ride and let him go to the winds on one of the ridges outside of Jackman. I had just the right spot picked out, with sweeping views of the mountain and lakes in all directions. He would have loved it.

The problem was remembering he was back there, waiting in his box under the seat. You see, every time I'd get geared up for a ride from Spruce Meadow, or the Border Riders clubhouse, or anywhere else in the state for that matter, I'd be so excited to go that I'd roar off down the trail and completely forget that he was still in the truck. An entire season went by without me getting my act together to finally lay him to rest and I admit it got to be kind of a joke among us. The summer went on with him still in his box, and then the fall. It got to the point where someone would get in the backseat and I'd suggest they say hello to Tarzan, which was met with varying degrees of disgust and discomfort.

The winter of 2017, I finally decided to take the turn from ITS 87 and run up Coburn Mountain. I had passed by this on earlier trips and kept hearing that the ride up, and view from the top, were good. A friend and I shot up it one day in January and, while it was cloudy that day and there was zero visibility, it occurred to me that this would be a good spot for the old hound dog. Would have been, that is, had I remembered to grab the box from the back of the truck. James and I continued on our way past Parlin Pond, rolling over to The Birches Resort for lunch before heading back to the Park and Ride at The Forks, but all the while I knew I had found my, or rather Tarzan's, spot.

I was back in Jackman just a few weeks later, with Eben this time. The first day we spent east of town, finding our way to the

Chesuncook Lake House and back, and looking for pieces of Eben's windshield after he rolled over going up a skidder cut. Chesuncook Lake House is arguably the most remote of all the fuel-and-food stops I've come across in Maine. It's accessible, barely, by logging road, boat, or seaplane. It's a bucket list item for any fan of the North Woods, and I bet it's just as cool in summer as it is in winter. (Sadly, in March 2018, the Lake House burned and was a total loss. The owners have been working to rebuild it from the ground up.) The second day, after stopping for a new windshield and belt for Eben's RMK, we headed for Coburn Mountain. Miraculously, I had finally remembered to put Tarzan in the storage compartment on my Ski-Doo. Today was his big day.

This was the second week of February and the week before school vacation, so the trails hadn't been too crowded and the riding was superb. It's always nice to have the trails to yourself, and we took our time going south from Jackman, ducking onto skidder roads and enjoying fresh tracks where we could. After lunch at Lake Parlin Lodge, it was time for the ride up Coburn, and I was eager to see the view when the top wasn't in the clouds. We peeled off the ITS and I was encouraged to see tracks going up.

The trail up Coburn Mountain is narrow, winding, and steep. Members of the local club, Coburn Summit Riders, occasionally groom halfway up and from there they plow out the drifts, but it's too narrow and steep to bring the drag all the way up. This mountain is well over 3,000 feet high and gets a lot of wind, so having someone bust out drifts ahead of you is extremely helpful. Naturally, I was anticipating no issues, and that was the case for nearly a mile. There's a little opening in a hollow at this point where the groomer leaves its drag and this point was also where the fresh tracks of two

Tarzan's tree.

previous riders had turned around. The trail continued on, fresh snow untracked and beckoning like a siren of the sea. We would be breaking trail on our own from here on out.

Innocently, we went on, encountering no problems at first until we rounded the corner for the last pitch leading to the summit. Half a foot of new snow from the night before had all blown into the trail at this height and had formed into wind-packed snowdrifts. Big ones. What had been a pleasant, mildly bumpy ride turned instantly into a horror show. Five- and six-foot-high drifts lasting for ten feet dropped off suddenly to bare ground and then immediately soared back to vertically walled drifts. All this at the top of a mountain, on a thirty-degree incline.

There was no way to keep momentum, as any speed would launch us off the drifts onto frozen rocks and dirt, and then—assuming we could have landed upright on the sleds—we would instantly have rammed into the next huge drift. All I can say is that we tried. We tried hard for a full two hours, and at the end of that, we had gained less than one hundred feet more of the trail. We'd get one sled stuck, dig it out and onto the packed snow, then pin the throttle and go for the next one, only to get mired once more. Then we'd leave the lead sled steaming contentedly in its new drift, slide back down the trail to the other sled, and do it all over again. Mind you, both of our sleds are highly capable, medium- to long-track sleds, with big paddles, driven by two motivated and strong guys, and we got our butts totally handed to us that afternoon.

Soaked with sweat, pissed off and disgusted, realizing we'd reached our limit, I announced that Tarzan would be just fine here, two hundred feet from the top. There was no disagreement from Eben. I carved a big "T" into one of the dwarf pines and grabbed the small wooden container from the back of my sled. Truth be told, this was the first time I had opened the box from the vet. Holding up the plastic bag of tiny white gravel pieces, I grimly realized that I was looking at his bones. With a heavy heart, I carried it up to the top of the nearest drift and looked around at the view, Sugarloaf off to the southwest and Moosehead to the east. It was a good spot for an old hound.

I had thought I would open the bag and fling his ashes in a big arc, majestically spreading him to the four corners of the compass. But when I drew my arm back to start the fling, my foot suddenly plunged through the top of the drift and I collapsed straight down and backward a little bit. The bag snagged on my finger and dumped its contents all over the drift, and all over me. I'm afraid I said some things about Tarzan on the top of that mountain that I shouldn't have, but it is true that he had the last laugh and would have liked that.

I always stay at the same place when I'm in the Jackman area. Spruce Meadow Cabins are tiny and adequately equipped, and they have hot running water. They can get cramped with more than two people, and it would be nice if the bathroom had a ceiling, or the Wi-Fi worked a bit better, but honestly, I'm not looking for too many creature comforts while snowmobiling. Just getting back to a warm cabin and a cold beer can feel pretty darn good after 150 miles of cold and wind. That these particular cabins are a couple of miles out of town is nice too.

At the beginning of each day, after the groomers have been out all night, the trails are wonderfully flat. However, the sheer amount of snowmobile traffic from any given winter day in Jackman leaves the town trails roughed up with moguls and divots. Staying just out of town and so close to the ITS means you don't have to worry about the mess in town. The owner of these cabins is an avid and accomplished rider, and I pick his brain every chance I get about what sleds to ride, where to ride, when to ride there, the local weather, groomer schedules, moose sheds, and countless unnamed places to go to. True to Mainer form, getting anything out of him is like pulling teeth. When inquiring about directions to faraway places I've offered beer, money, and lobsters, but I may as well have offered a stick in the eye. Usually it goes like so:

"What's the best way to the St. John Ponds?"

"Why would you want to go there?"

"I've never been and I like that sort of thing."

"You know the groomer was out last night? Trails will be mint."

"Yah, but I've ridden all these trails. I haven't been to those ponds."

"Well, that stuff is really just for us guys around here . . . "

"How about some lobsters?"

"Yah . . . No thanks."

"Ever thought about guiding sled trips?"

"Yes, I have thought about that, and I decided not to."

And so on from there. But I'm working on him. I can be a persistent bugger when I put my mind to it, and I can see a time when he'll suggest I tag along for a ride in the backcountry. Probably in about twenty years.

◆ Recommended Ride

From The Forks it's an easy, satisfying adventure to ride thirty or so miles over to Moosehead Lake and have lunch at The Birches Resort. This wonderful lodge is tucked along the shore of the big lake, two miles from Mount Kineo, and offers up spectacular views to its diners. Personally, I try to get here at least twice a winter. You can fuel up, warm up, eat up, and rest up here while knowing you have nothing but an easy ride home. The trails are famously well-marked so if directions aren't necessarily your thing, you'll still be okay. If you're making good time and the ice is thick enough, the local club will have a trail across the lake to Mount Kineo, usually marked with small pine trees every two hundred yards or so, frozen into the ice. The houses there will be boarded up for the winter, but it is well worth poking around.

Springfield

Grand Lake
Stream

Eastern Maine

Machias

Bar Harbor

Mount Desert
Island

5

Eastern
Maine

The interstate from Bangor to Houlton is 120 miles long and effectively defines the entire eastern region of Maine, particularly if you start just thirty miles south of Bangor at the mouth of Penobscot Bay. Over the years I've spent less than a dozen days riding in this part of the state. That isn't very much, and I know that I've hardly scratched the surface. It's vast, like the County, and anything but flat with plenty of 1,000-foot-high hills and long ridges. So far, I've felt that snowmobiling in Eastern Maine just has a different feel than anywhere else in the state. It's difficult to pinpoint exactly what the difference is. The trails are nearly always in excellent shape, well-groomed and marked, with great snow coverage. Sometimes more snow falls here than anywhere else in Maine. In 2015 Machias recorded more than ten feet in one five-week stretch! Maybe one of the differences is that there is never a crowd. You can put one hundred miles on the sled and pass just two or three other riders. Or it could be that, besides Route 1 and Route 9, there just aren't many major roads. In fact, the area around Grand Lake Stream is as wild and untouched as the outer reaches of the Allagash. No crowds and not many towns can be great for getting first tracks and trails all to yourself, but it means you have to plan

> No crowds and not many towns can be great for getting first tracks and trails all to yourself, but it means you have to plan carefully for fuel and lunch stops. It also helps if you know someone with a cabin.

carefully for fuel and lunch stops. It also helps if you know someone with a cabin.

Steve is an old friend of Dan and Carol's and his cabin sits high on a hill overlooking Upper Sysladobsis Lake. Dan had spent plenty of time up there years back, but after he sold his first round of sleds, nearly a decade went by without his having a chance to visit. When I was first grilling him about his old snowmobile haunts this was one of the places he always mentioned, and his description of the camp and surrounding area was nothing short of spellbinding. Having spent so many years crisscrossing the Gulf of Maine, I was thinking that maybe I had been missing out. Dan had been crisscrossing the state during the same time, but on a snowmobile, and I was jealous! In the winter of 2014 we were possessed of the Viper and the Renegade, and Dan happened to mention this to Steve at a Christmas party. That was all it took. A day or two after the Super Bowl, we were invited to ride in and stay a few nights, and it's safe to say we were both excited at the prospect. We were in for trouble, and didn't know it.

January of that year was the real deal. Blizzards, Arctic cold blasts, Alberta clippers—you name it and the state of Maine got it. One coastal storm after another hammered New England, and winter records were shattered everywhere. Monhegan recorded an unprecedented seven feet of snow in three back-to-back storms that month. I was tasked with plowing the island's two miles of unpaved roads and, after the second storm clobbered the island and with an eye to the next one bearing down on us, I bought the town a snowblower to push back the berms along the narrow dirt roads. One can only drive a truck about ten miles an hour on many of the small coastal islands, which means that the plow can't get the snow moving fast enough to really clear the shoulder of the roads, and so the snow just falls back in behind the plow truck as you make pass after pass. After the first three or four feet fell, there was just no place left to put the snow. That spring I learned that all the other islands had the same issue and had dealt with it in similar ways. It was a lot of fun if you like dealing with snow removal and things of this nature, which I do.

For whatever reason, I have always had a thing about plow trucks. I can remember the thrill of being woken up as a kid, at two in the morning, hearing the big dump trucks grinding by with their dual blades, rumbling on through a blizzard, only to wake up hours later to a snow day. I had managed to convince my mother that I should get fifty cents for every inch of snow I shoveled, a fact that still bothers my older brothers who had by then moved on. I'd shovel out the whole driveway and then go in for a cup of cocoa, only to be devastated when the plow would come along and bury the driveway back in.

But I loved to watch them. The local guys plowing driveways were also a source of wonder and, honestly, some jealousy. I can tell you, it got pretty rough on me, a young boy with no access whatso-ever to any heavy equipment. So, I did what any clever Maine kid would do. I made my own. I needed a vehicle and a plow, so I got my bicycle and a shovel, one of the wide ones, and I concocted a mechanism whereby I could pedal up a head of steam toward the driveway and, at the last second, pull a rope that would drop the shovel from its pivot point on the handlebars and engage the "plow."

I wasn't too good with ropes and knots at this point in my life. Invariably, the shovel would actually plow maybe two inches of the driveway, hit a frozen rock, snap the rope, and drive the end of the shovel into my gut, pitching me off the bike and knocking the wind out of me. God knows what people driving by thought of that crazy kid on the bike with a shovel flapping around the front tire, but let me tell you, if I could have bought a V-shaped shovel to mount on the front, I'd have been the talk of the town!

Anyhow, Maine got a lot of snow the year that I was first invited to Steve's camp. In fact, he reported so much snow when he got to his camp road that he never bothered to unload his sled from the trailer. He's got a short track Ski-Doo, fan-cooled, no picks, and short paddles, and he knew full well he'd never make it more than twenty feet before he'd be buried in the four feet of snow that covered the logging road to his camp. He turned around and, knowing him as I do now, it must have been a tough call to make.

Steve loves that camp. It's an oasis for him. When he's there, life comes to a standstill and the everyday issues that plague us all are forgotten. What becomes important is getting the firewood in and unfrozen, keeping the massive pot of water on to melt snow, planning and preparing three meals a day, monitoring the inevitably plummeting temperatures and impending doomsday storm. I can hear him gleefully exclaiming, "You boys gonna have a cold ride today!" while enjoying his first stogie of the day, usually accompanied by the first cocktail. These are things he busies himself with at camp, and I admit I'm jealous.

So, when he realized he couldn't get in there, he turned around for home and put in a call to Dan. I don't know just how the conversation went, but the upshot was that we would meet Steve in three days' time and somehow break out the six-mile trail in to his camp. I didn't have nearly enough experience to be as concerned as I should have been.

When we arrived in Springfield, which is ten miles past Lee, which is ten miles past Lincoln, Steve was there to meet us and tell us where we could leave our truck and trailer. This was my first time meeting him, but Dan had filled me in on his sense of humor and I was ready for it. After trading a few jabs and catching up on the big game, we got to discussing the job ahead of us. There was a lot of head shaking and frowning coming from Steve and his buddy Jeff, a local gentleman who was, apparently, going with us. They had been waiting around that afternoon and had tried to go a little ways on their own, only to get promptly stuck, and had decided they'd better wait for help. They seemed generally happy to see me. It still hadn't dawned on me that I was the youngest one of the group by twenty years and that my youth would soon be put to good use.

I should say here that my sled, of the four that were lined up for the ride in, was maybe the least capable for the conditions we were in for. Not that the other sleds were new off-trail mountain sleds by any means, but still the short track Viper was out of its element that afternoon. I didn't let it bother me much. If these three old guys were going, I was going with them. The lineup went like this: Dan on his Renegade, then Steve on his newer fan-cooled Ski-Doo towing a jet sled mounded over with gear and coolers, then Jeff on a borrowed short-track Polaris, and I brought up the rear, also towing a jet sled of beer, backpacks, sleeping bags, and other miscellaneous pieces of gear.

I noticed a funny thing as we got ourselves situated. Steve, Dan, and I all had adequate riding gear including helmets, coats, bibs, and most importantly, I observed, gloves. This rough-looking fellow Jeff, though . . . he didn't appear worried that he was in jeans, with a threadbare army jacket, tattered Mad Bomber hat, and no gloves, just thin glove liners. I shrugged it off, as one sees many strange things in the backwoods of Maine and I supposed this was just how he rode snowmobiles. I certainly wasn't about to suggest he was pushing his luck and so minded my own business.

About four in the afternoon, with the sun sinking behind the trees, we fired up the sleds and headed out. Any time you head out on a new trail, in a new area, it's exciting. I wasn't too worried tooling along at the back of the pack. The three sleds ahead of me were pushing through pretty well and packing in a nice trail for me. I had to pay attention, mind you, but it was good going as far as I was concerned. For about five minutes. Dan had gotten out of sight ahead of us, as he knew he'd need to keep his speed up to blast through all the snow. The first sign of trouble I saw was the brake lights from the two sleds still in sight. We stopped in a line and when I walked up to have a look at the holdup, I started laughing. Dan's sled was fully buried down in a ditch on the right side of the road.

"I don't know what happened. I just started drifting right and then I was in it."

"Looks like you didn't even try to turn!"

"Well, I did, but nothing happened. Where's the shovel?"

At the last minute when we were loading the jet sleds, I had tossed a snow shovel on top and lashed it down. This would turn out to be one of the most fortuitous things I've ever done, but also one of the most regrettable. I returned to Dan's sled with the shovel and, while Steve and Dan discussed the route in and the various turns that needed to be taken at which landmarks, I shoveled out the

Renegade. Jeff had a few smokes and looked around. Soon enough, Dan was underway again and I had almost gotten back to my sled when I realized I couldn't hear anything. In particular, I couldn't hear the sound of Dan's two-stroke rocketing off into the fading light. I whipped around and was shocked to see him just one hundred yards farther down the snowed-in logging road, bottomed out again in the right-hand ditch.

The three of us trudged up and I could hear the concern in Steve's voice. Not because Dan's sled was buried in the ditch, again, but because he was convinced we had gone as far as we were going to go. His time to be at camp was dwindling, and so were his hopes. We repeated the scene from moments before, complete with route discussions and gazing around and one of us shoveling. This time Dan announced his intention to stand up on the sled as he rode and thus use his body weight to help steer the sled in the deep snow. By leaning to the left or right, it is possible to "drift" a snowmobile around corners. Skilled mountain riders do this all day long. Dan took off into the now-dark night while the three of us shook our heads and returned to our sleds. For better or worse, we were committed to following him.

Steve and Jeff fired up and drove off into the night, lights fading, as I took a breather. It wasn't a cold night, in the twenties, and I was getting a bit soggy from sweat. I wasn't upset. Quite the opposite. Alone, sitting sideways on the Viper, I looked up and could see about a million stars. It was quiet, and I was pleased to be where I was in the world as I cooled down. We had started out at four and according to my phone it was nearly six. Two hours to go a mile! Another few minutes of peace and I got going, careful to not get out of the fresh track laid out ahead of me—almost a tunnel, really—and to stay mindful of the jet sled I was towing.

Dan with a very buried Renegade.

At this point, I couldn't go around the next corner without thinking I'd see the other three huddled up on the trail ahead of me, sleds steaming into the night air, waiting for the shovel or young muscle or both. But the farther I went the more encouraged I got. It helped that it was a night ride. I only ride at night four or five times a winter, and it's always great. I don't know why we don't do it more often. Monitoring the mileage on the dash of the Yamaha, I got to a mile and still hadn't caught up with them. Then another mile, and a third, and then there they were.

Dan had stopped at a "Y" in the road and wasn't sure which way to go. (So much for all the route mapping an hour before, although in his defense it *had* been years since he was in this neck of the woods.) Luckily, no one was stuck, and they were just waiting to make sure I was good before the final push to camp. I asked Steve how close we were, and the excitement was clear in his voice. Less than two miles. Admonishing Dan to remember the hard left at the gravel pit, we unhitched the two jet sleds as there were several uphill sections coming and we thought it would be best to pack the trail down and come back for them.

Ten minutes later we were at the gravel pit. At least, four people were there. But sleds, I only saw three.

"Dan, where in hell is your sled?"

"Under those trees over there."

I looked around and finally saw his Renegade; he had driven through and under a thicket of small pines.

"I didn't see the gravel pit until I was right next to it and by then I was going too fast to make the turn."

"No kidding."

At the last second, he had taken the turn, at speed, and didn't quite have the room to pull it off. He said it took him five minutes just to get *himself* out, partly because he was laughing so hard. Managing the extraction of the Renegade took all of us, and my trusty shovel. The small trees that were jammed through the skis and the track compounded the problem. I'm afraid we demolished a fair amount of promising young timber in the process. It was the deepest hole yet. Going once more, we proceeded up a long hill with some fresh moose tracks. (I was actually quite concerned with those tracks that night; with my short track and the deep snow I had no way of escaping one of the big fellows if he took a liking to me.) At last we pulled into an opening in the woods revealing a cabin and several outbuildings.

Steve was thrilled. There was a lot of backslapping as we all piled into the cabin and had a look around. Dan was the clear hero of the journey but, true to form, he shrugged it off as just another ride in the woods. Steve lit the propane heater while Jeff got the woodstove going. He had set a chair directly in front of the stove, and it seemed clear that he wasn't too keen on moving. I suggested two of us go back for the jet sleds full of, among other less necessary items, all the beer. The trip back out of camp was a breeze. What had taken us an hour just a few moments ago now took only ten minutes, and soon we were piling back into the clearing. We dug out a case of beer, and I can tell you it was easily the most refreshing one I have ever had. Four hours to go six miles, and worth every bit of it.

The next day we spent exploring the area, or at least what we could of it. Where the club had groomed, we had no problems and no company. I don't believe we ever saw another sled that first day. Once, we did attempt to continue on a trail that hadn't seen a groomer in several weeks and the untracked snow was just too tempting for me. I blasted off across a field and was able to keep the Viper going, albeit with the throttle wide open to prevent me from sinking into stuck-ville. When the field narrowed into a wooded trail, I was forced to slow down and that did me in. Dan was patiently following and helped me get turned around. We both knew it was foolish to keep going as we'd spend all day getting stuck and digging out.

Late that night we were just finishing up one of Steve's home-cooked extravaganzas when we heard two sleds pull up. They belonged to Brian and Dave, two of Steve's work friends who were annual visitors to his camp. They were sufficiently impressed with the trail we had broken in and were amazed at the amount of snow.

In the morning Steve announced that we had a rescue mission to undertake. His camp was part of an association of land and camp owners. He had received a call from a retired couple living completely off the grid, just a few miles away. They were snowbound and, though they had a snowmobile, the woman had snowshoed out from the house half a mile or so and deemed it too deep for them to try to get out on their own. They had heard the whine of our sleds as we were working our way in the first night and now asked if we could pack down the trail to their house. Of course, Steve said yes. We were all interested to see the compound as he informed us it was a beautiful spot that they had picked for their retirement. We geared up and rode down to the "Y" in the road where we had left the jet sleds on our way in and took a left. I don't know who was leading the pack, but I know I was last, because a moment later I got stuck and there was no one behind me to lend a hand. I finally managed to dig out, unfairly disgusted with my little lake racer and myself. I caught up with the group at the house.

The couple were pleased to see us. They insisted we come in for coffee and a warm-up, which we did, all marveling at the simple elegance and ingenuity of the dwelling. It was one of those houses that makes you instantly envious and leaves you wondering why you couldn't be smart enough to come up with the ideas they had. The gentleman told us that late in the fall, around Thanksgiving or so, they usually do a last big shopping trip in Lincoln and stock up on necessities, including prescriptions, but this year, with all the snow, they were overdue by several weeks for another "town run" and were perilously close to running out of some things. They had plenty of firewood, and thus heat, and the well ran off of solar with a generator backup, so they were comfortable enough but, as anyone would be in their situation, they were getting nervous halfway through a rugged Maine winter. Steve was pleased we were able to help them out, and we were all impressed with how and where they had chosen to live. I often think back to those two living halfway up on the south side of a hill, surrounded by forest and looking out over their garden and valley. One could do a lot worse.

Back at the "Y" in the trail, Steve turned back for camp (*gotta get dinner going*) and Dan and I accompanied Brian and Dave for an afternoon ride. They knew the area much better than we did, though we all had the same problems with snow depth. There were just too many tempting logging roads with untouched powder. I don't recall seeing any other riders, and we put down mile after mile of fresh tracks through the forests and fields. It was an afternoon of riding that sticks with you, and all your worries fade away, and you recognize that time stands still for just long enough, sometimes.

A bluebird day in Eastern Maine.

It was about at this point when I realized that, for me, snowmobiling has something in common with downhill skiing. Ever since I worked at Sugarloaf, my absolute favorite time to ski has been during or just after a fresh snowfall. Fresh tracks is a term that all skiers know and something many seek out. There was always a competition with the ski patrol to lay down fresh tracks on the best trails, and we snowmakers had plenty of tricks to ensure those tracks were ours. Whether or not we accomplished this within the rules of the mountain was immaterial to us, and it developed into an ongoing contest that was almost as much fun as the skiing.

It turns out I have the same attitude about riding. When faced with a field or trail with untouched snow, I have an overwhelming desire to go make tracks on it. In fact, the urge often overpowers any sense of logic and the knowledge that, at least in the Viper days, I'd end up stuck. It's an almost irresistible feeling, and now that I'm on the long-track Backcountry it's only gotten more fun to seek these areas out.

There is, however, an issue in the industry around this attitude. Many trails in the state run over privately owned land, and landowners are incredibly generous about letting clubs access these areas with connecting trails. As long as riders stay on the marked trails, there are no issues. But every now and then some fool goes tearing off across a field that he shouldn't be on, invariably runs over a fledgling raspberry patch or tree farm and ruins it, causing the landowner to be furious and lose his last shred of patience. There is no excuse for it. With a little planning and gas, seeking out untracked areas is actually easy and, in my experience, all part of the fun. A little creativity goes a long way toward feeding this addiction, and when you do find your own secret stashes you'll start to guard their whereabouts when chatting with other riders. Indeed, if I see a pack of long-track mountain sleds, I try to avoid talking with the riders so I won't have to lie about where I've just come from. I would expect the same from them and it's amazing how vague the directions can get.

> Many trails in the state run over privately owned land, and landowners are incredibly generous about letting clubs access these areas with connecting trails. As long as riders stay on the marked trails, there are no issues.

"Well, you go back up the trail about five, maybe ten, miles? You'll see a birch tree followed by a small rock and then you go a bit farther. Take the right—was it a right, Timmy? Anyhow the trail splits and if you go out one of the trails another few miles, you come to a four corners, and then from there . . . "

And on and on until the poor guy's ears are bleeding. It's all in good fun, and as I've been lucky enough to be taken along to friends' powder stashes, so too am I guilty of showing off the goods.

One night at Steve's camp we were sitting around after a day of riding, warming up and eagerly anticipating one of his famous dinners. The topic of discussion was riding, and I was comparing notes with Dave about various trips and the merits of lodging and restaurants to be found. Just a few days before, I had been reading about the Down East Sunrise Trail, connecting Ellsworth with Machias, and I mentioned this was on my list of trips to take.

"If there's enough snow to ride in Ellsworth you should try to ride on MDI while you're at it."

"You mean Bar Harbor?"

"Yup. I've heard of guys riding the Park Loop Road."

This surprising tidbit stayed with me and stayed close to the front of my mind. I was intrigued by the idea of it and aware that, given the right conditions, it would undoubtedly be spectacular. I am continually amazed at the places where snowmobilers manage to drive their sleds. I once saw, somewhere around Millinocket, if memory serves, a picture from the 1980s of two old Ski-Doos perched atop Mount Katahdin. I have no idea how this was managed but it sure looked real to me.

Dave didn't have much information about riding on Mount Desert Island (MDI) as he had never done it himself, but I had a connection that I thought might be able to shed some light on it for me. I knew the head brewer at Atlantic Brewing, on MDI, was an avid hiker and I suspected he knew the area as well as or better than most.

Located mainly on MDI, Acadia National Park has been around for more than a century and is rightfully one of the most popular national parks in the country. Similar to Baxter State Park, Acadia is open to snowmobiles but does not groom any roads or trails. The Park Loop Road is an incredibly scenic twenty-seven-mile-long mostly one-way road, making stops at the famed Sand Beach and Thunder Hole, then on past Jordan Pond, finally winding itself up to the top of Cadillac Mountain. From here you can see the sun rise before anyone else on the east coast of the United States, assuming you wake up early enough. Bar Harbor may be one of the busiest, most-visited spots in Maine during the summer months but, like so much of our coast, in the winter it is a quiet and unassuming oceanside town. Firing question after question to my brewing acquaintance, I learned that the Park Loop Road is not plowed in the winter and there is a winter parking lot at Hulls Cove Visitor Center, the park's main entrance. Good enough for me.

Several weeks later, just after a nor'easter blasted through leaving upward of two feet of snow in its wake, I was off. I had done my research, although there was little enough information about it, and had just been waiting for the right time to go. I figured that since I'd be riding on unplowed pavement, a foot of snow would be a sufficient depth and this latest storm had doubled that. I had my GPS and a full tank of gas, and I figured I'd just go scout it out and see how I fared. This was a solo trip so I loaded my sled in the back of the truck and left the trailer at home.

From Liberty it was less than a two-hour drive to Hulls Cove. I pulled in and the first thing I saw were three empty trucks in the lot and three sets of fresh snowmobile tracks leading out around the gate to the Park Loop Road. Normally I would be disappointed to see that I wouldn't have fresh tracks but a little part of my brain suggested it might be good to have tracks to follow since I was new here. In fact, I probably hadn't been to Thunder Hole in twenty-five years, since childhood, so this was a good case of better safe than sorry. I backed the truck up to a snowbank, reversed the Backcountry off onto it, geared up, and took off.

Going around the gate to enter the park, I was instantly on edge. There was more snow than I had thought there would be, and I'd have to be careful not to get mired. Believe it or not, there are times when it seems like there's too *much* snow and this was one of those times. Had I been on a true long track, and were I a bit more athletic and balanced, these would have been absolutely ideal conditions. As it was, the going was good but challenging, and I needed to focus. There were three sleds ahead of me, and I figured I'd just go wherever they led me.

Before long, the road turned toward the coast on the northeast side of the island and hugged the shoreline. The view was as expected. Looking over Frenchman's Bay was stunning, and I stopped at Thunder Hole to snap a few pictures. The road here was so close to the ocean that sea spray had turned the snow slushy and left the ground almost bare in places open to the wind.

I was still following the tracks as I rounded Otter Cove and they looked fresh, even just minutes old. I guessed I was less than an hour behind them, and when I stopped to take pictures I kept expecting to hear them out ahead of me, but I never did. I wasn't exactly lost at this point, but nothing looked too familiar. Looking at the map afterward (typical for me) I realized there were two roads going around the island. With the fresh snow, any landmarks I might have recognized from years ago were none too obvious. Rounding a corner into a seemingly random set of horse stables, I finally came upon the other riders. There were several small fields around the buildings, and two of the riders were horsing around, doing doughnuts and slaloming this way and that. The third was taking a breather, and I drove right up to him as he sat there enjoying a smoke. We chatted as first one and then the other rider came up to see who the new guy was. We all agreed it was tremendous riding, and I admitted I was glad they had laid down tracks ahead of me as I had never ridden here.

They were locals, of course, and at first, they were surprised to hear that I had come from Monhegan. I explained about Liberty and said I was here mostly on a whim and, if they didn't mind, I'd just tag along. Being good Maine boys, they said sure, probably aware that if they said no I'd just give them a head start and follow along regardless.

Two of them rode Polaris sleds and the other was on a Yamaha, and it quickly became evident they were good riders and knew the area. We blasted through the woods on the unplowed roads and never saw any other signs of life. The new snow glistened on every rock and tree. It was untouched and we had it all to ourselves. With the sun shining and a steady northwest breeze, it felt comfortable, and right, to be mounted on a snowmobile with no destination and no clock. I realized it was to be one of those days that helps snowmobilers get through the summer. You think back on all the days spent on snow and compare the ones that stand out, and then realize it's only early August, and you sigh and go back to daydreaming.

We stopped at Eagle Lake, but the ice had a funny look to it and we left it alone. Cadillac Mountain was next, and I had my doubts about it. The road up Cadillac, from what I could remember, was steep and possessed of numerous switchbacks. Because the road is partly on the southwest side of the mountain, I was positive that it would be totally buried from the recent nor'easter. Letting my imagination get the better of me for a minute, I saw myself not making the turn on a switchback and tumbling over the side, helmet flying off, sled pitch-poling through the air, scattering myself and my sled across a thousand feet of granite.

"So the turnoff for Cadillac is off the road we came in on, right?"

"Yah, but it'll be fine. Easy ride up to the top."

"Uh-huh. If you don't see me behind you guys don't worry . . . I may skip it."

The three of them probably weren't too impressed with my courage level, but let me tell you, imagination can be a powerful thing. We shot the breeze for a bit longer, discussing previous rides and sleds, and then we were off. I brought up the rear again, not wanting to hold them up, and just as we were nearing the turnoff to go up the mountain, I saw the Yamaha ahead of me stop. The burly rider opened the port side cowling. I pulled up to him as the first two riders circled back and we all walked over for a look at the ailing sled. The drive belt was starting to go and he had heard the first shreds of it banging around in the engine compartment. He had no spare. He also wouldn't be going up any mountains with a belt in that condition. His day was done and he knew it.

Using my knife, he cut off the stray fronds of rubber and said he'd just try to idle the sled back to the parking lot. Suddenly I realized that my worries about flying off the side of a mountain were unnecessary. His pals would accompany him back to the trucks and, of course, tow him in if the half-shredded belt came completely apart. None of us were going up Cadillac now.

Given the condition of that belt, we were all surprised he made it the five miles back and I'm sure he was scowling into his helmet as the three of us danced around him on our sleds, enjoying the powder while he motored along just above an idle. I said thanks to them after we were all loaded up, traded business cards with one of them, and no doubt I'll see them again next year, same place, doing the same thing. Hopefully that Yamaha guy brings a spare belt.

◆ Recommended Ride

The last ride, of 2018, for Dan and me was one of my favorite rides, ever. We both managed to squeeze into our schedules a single day off for riding, and we left Liberty thinking we'd try the Sunrise Trail out of Ellsworth. For some reason we ended up thirty miles east of there on the Airline Road, also known as Route 9. We were both a bit on the skeptical side as we pulled into the parking lot of the Airline Lodge in Beddington. We needn't have been. The owner was backing his trail groomer into a large canvas tent, and he told us he had just done his last run of the season with it. He told us where we could park, suggested a ride to Grand Lake Stream and back, and then he was off to tackle his next project. After gearing up and heading out we were thrilled to find flat, wide trails with no one on them. There wasn't a cloud in the sky, and we flew off into the unfamiliar, after a while crossing the Stud Mill Road and then stopping at a gorgeous, deserted public campsite on Unknown Lake. We saw a group of three riders coming the other way at one point, and those would turn out to be the only other snowmobilers we saw for the entire day. Just as I was getting hungry, we coasted into town, crossing the southern end of West Grand Lake, and pulled into the general store for fuel and a bite to eat. Walking into the Pine Tree Store, the first thing you notice is fish and fishing gear. Maps of the local waterways, mounted brookies and salmon, poles, reels, baskets, and vests adorn the walls, and the entire middle of a back room is devoted to various fly lures. The proprietor informed us that it was quiet now at the end of March but it wouldn't last much longer. Fishing season opens in Maine on April 1 and the Grand Lake Stream area is one the state's hot spots for early-season fanatics. After a perfect lunch (I had finally learned that I didn't have to eat *everything* on the plate) we retraced our route from that morning and I was pleased with our decision to try someplace new. Knowing it was my last ride of the season, I couldn't resist some untracked logging roads and so I zoomed off on a couple of them. Both led to dead ends a few miles in, as they often do. We arrived back at the trailer in Beddington late that afternoon and were soon on our way back to the farm in Liberty. It was a superb ending to a great season of riding.

Estcourt
Station

Madawaska

Fort Kent

Allagash

Wallagrass

Caribou

The County

6

The County

With more than seven thousand square miles of hills, fields, rivers, lakes, farms, and endless timber country, Maine's Aroostook County is by far the largest county in the state, bigger than Rhode Island and Connecticut combined. Known as "the County" by most everybody in New England, Aroostook is annually rated as one of the top five snowmobile destinations in the United States.

Aroostook is a Native American word meaning "beautiful river," and it's hard to know just which river they might have been referring to. There's the Fish River, the St. Croix River, the Penobscot River, the Big Black River, the Allagash, the mighty St. John, the Aroostook, and more. They are all unique and all have played roles in Maine's history. However, there is much more to the County than rivers. The farms of Aroostook are known far and wide for their potatoes. Indeed, thousands of acres are dedicated to the growing of spuds and, famously, the grade schools are on full recess during harvest, allowing all hands on deck to pick the crop. (Every year when I ride in the County, I forget to buy myself a bag of County potatoes. Five dollars for a fifty-pound bag is hard to beat. Someday I'll remember.)

Recently, some of the younger generation of Aroostook farmers have invested time and money in the growing of barley, which is then

Snow ratios are excellent in the County. That is to say, the colder the air, the more snow you can squeeze out of a storm's moisture. All that cold air that hangs around the crown of Maine means that while the rest of the state is getting rain, it's snowing up north.

malted and used as the workhorse ingredient in beer. Maine is home to more than one hundred craft breweries, and many of them are proud to use grain from the County in their beer. Logging is also prevalent here, with more than fifty large operations and many smaller affairs too numerous to count. Wood products have always been a mainstay of the state and the universities offer programs and degrees dedicated to the responsible, safe harvest of Maine's timber resource. Many flatlanders, myself included, are often seen with mouths agape, staring at the endless rows of logs waiting for processing and the massive machines used to harvest them.

Aroostook County is home to much of Maine's best hunting and fishing and, therefore, many of the state's most accomplished guides. Even the title Registered Maine Guide is so rich in history and ability that it instantly evokes respect. White-tailed deer are somewhat less common in northern Maine than in the southern part of the state, but few would deny that the woods and fields here are home to the biggest bucks in the Northeast. Moose roam pretty much wherever they please, and most folks are delighted to brag about the monster bull strolling down Main Street. Hunting and fishing opportunities are endless here, and the quest for trophy fish gets fulfilled many times over.

Aroostook County is also home to long, long winters. The leaves often are turning early in September, the first snow arrives in

October, ice is forming in November, and by the time December rolls around, any thoughts of warm summer breezes by the lake are distant memories. But Old Man Winter is only getting started. Winter is fully upon the County for nearly six months a year, with November and April capable of producing big snows and deep cold snaps. The record low temperature for the state is a nasty fifty below zero, recorded at the Big Black River checkpoint deep in the Allagash. Folks in the County get used to it, if they aren't born into it, and I often wonder if they start to relish the misery of a twenty-day stretch that never gets near the freezing mark, let alone above it. All this cold weather helps with snow, both producing it and then keeping it around. The County averages ninety inches of snow a season, almost eight feet if you're counting, and every year seems to set some new record for snowfall. In 2016 the record set was for having at least a foot of snow on the ground for four straight months.

Statistics are certainly interesting to look at, but we know they don't tell the whole story. I have heard some locals speak of snow produced by the St. Lawrence River. Cold northwest wind blowing across the river picks up moisture, turns it to snow, and drops it in the North Woods, similar to lake effect snow. Whether or not this is true, I don't know, but I like the sound of it. One aspect of the region that is true: It's usually so cold there that the snow ratios are excellent. That is to say, the colder the air, the more snow you can squeeze out of a storm's moisture. So, while the average snowfall may be one thing in the south, one hundred miles north in the Allagash, it's another thing entirely. All that cold air that hangs around the crown of Maine means that while the rest of the state is getting rain, it's snowing up north.

For snowmobilers, it's heaven on earth. There are so many places

There are so many places to ride in Aroostook County, it is hard to know where to begin. Fortunately, you can't go wrong. There are more than forty clubs spread across the area, and they are highly regarded in their ability and management of trails.

to ride in Aroostook County, it is hard to know where to begin. Fortunately, you can't go wrong. There are more than forty clubs spread across the area, and they are highly regarded in their ability and management of trails. I have been lucky enough to ride here four of the years I've been going, and I feel I have barely scratched the surface. For instance, I have never ridden south of a line connecting Portage and Presque Isle. This includes the areas around Ashland, Patten, Houlton, and Mars Hill, respectively. Many would regard this region, basically all of southern Aroostook County, as the finest riding in Maine. I have never ridden in the far western reaches of the County either. This area never sees a groomer and is so remote that most riders never have, or will, or even want to, explore it, leaving it to the logging outfits and wardens and a few remote sporting camps.

The second year I had the Viper was the first year I went to Aroostook County. Dan was adamant that we go, recalling his past excursions, and of course it didn't take much convincing for me to be on board. Having arranged for a cabin at the aptly named Caribou Cabins, located right on the ITS, we departed late in February from Liberty. We were against it from the get-go—a full gale of wind (fifty mph) out of the northeast, for two hundred miles. The drive became a series of pit stops as our miles per gallon plummeted. Between the wind coming at us head on and the trailer we were towing, we had to stop three times for gas.

North of Millinocket, it was all new to me and I loved it. Interstate 95 ends in Houlton and becomes Route 1 from here, and along each side were snowbanks ten feet tall where front-end loaders had been pushing the drifts off the side of the road. When we finally arrived at the cabin, the wind was blowing some recent snow up in the air, it was bitterly cold, the parking lot was full of ice and snow, and the sun was setting. The whole area had a feeling of desolation and resembled pictures of the frozen tundra—which, in a way, it was. Sometimes you imagine a place being the definition of a season, and this cabin was fulfilling its duty nicely with regard to winter.

In the morning, while waiting for Dan to get geared up (*What's he waiting for? Spring?*) I fired up the trusty Yamaha and, while circling the parking lot, was pleased to find an ITS connector one hundred feet from the front door, as promised. Truth in advertising is a rare thing. The wind was still cranking and, just as the cold was starting to seep through my gear, out came Dan and off we went. Sort of. Less than a mile from the cabin, still trying to figure out just where we were going, we drove around a corner and found a big pine blown down across the freshly groomed trail. It was a seventy-footer or so and completely blocked our way. By jumping up and down on the branches we managed to break enough to attempt going over the trunk, which we did, apparently without any damage.

Thinking we were in the clear, Dan ripped the pull cord on his sled. Nothing happened. He pulled again, and nothing happened. *To be fair*, it wasn't nothing. Every time he pulled, the engine would sluggishly roll over, give a low rumble from its cylinders, and then subside. After twenty or so pulls, by both of us, we figured something major must be wrong. After all, it had *just* been running. Trying to get cell service by holding the phone up to the sky and darting one way and then another, Dan was able to reach his mechanic back home. Of course, I only heard one end of the conversation, but I imagined it went something like:

"Try the what?"

"Try replacing the ignition fuse."

"What the heck is the rendition cue?"

"No, I said try putting a new fuse in the ignition."

"Sorry, what was the first part? I'm way up in the County, you see."

"I SAID RELACE THE IGNITION FUSE!"

"Oh right. Okay, thanks."

Reception isn't great up there, and I was smirking in my helmet. We put a new fuse in and the thing started right up. Finally, I thought to myself, we can get some riding in. About two miles. Launching onto one of the wide-open fields the County is so famous for, I was leading and trying to figure out how we'd get to Portage for lunch. Dan caught up to me at the next stop sign and, reaching over from his sled, handed me a small silver-and-black disk. We opened our helmets to talk.

"What's this?"

"That's one of your bogey wheels."

"Oh, I see. Bogey wheel. Mine, you say?"

"Yup. Flew off your sled when you pinned it coming across the field."

"Hmm."

"Can't ride without them, you know . . ."

I unseated myself and had a look. What I was in the process of learning was that there are two pulleys at the back end of a snowmobile that the rubber track turns on. They are bolted to the frame and allow the track to remain taut as the engine turns it, providing forward movement, and they are also meant to keep the track within its guides and ease the friction caused by the track going around endlessly. Basically, they are big bearings. And I was holding one of them in my hands.

It occurred to me that driving over the tree a mile back probably had something to do with this coming off. I hadn't realized anything was wrong, but we hadn't gone very far, either. Suddenly, the day was looking dark. Nine in the morning and we had already seen a trail issue, and a balky sled, and now this. We needed to find a Yamaha dealer. While I sat there despondently, Dan perused the County trail map and noticed one of its sponsors was Gary's Yamaha in Caribou. It had trail access and was less than a mile away! The dark cloud hanging over me thinned a little bit.

We pulled into a parking lot full of tractors, utility vehicles, and a wonderful row of new Yamaha snowmobiles. With the bogey wheel in hand and the fate of the trip on the line, I walked in and handed it to the fellow at the counter. He looked at it and pronounced it as coming from a 2004 Viper, probably the SX, and said it'd be about an hour to fix. Suffice it to say, I was impressed that he could recognize the model and year just from looking at the part. It never occurred to me until later that he was watching us drive up in front of the store windows and so knew exactly what sled the bogey wheel came from.

As they worked on my sled, we picked their brains about trails and fuel stops and they told us anything and everything we wanted to know. This was my first experience with anything snowmobile-related in the County, and it turned out to be a prelude to nearly every other interaction I've had while spending time there. Those boys at Gary's set the bar high for customer service.

An hour later we were off, for good this time. Besides seeing the open fields, rail beds, and superwide and perfectly groomed trails, only a few other things happened of note on this trip. Later that afternoon, about ten miles outside of Portage, I rounded a corner and found a coyote loping along the trail in front of me. Being the excitable sort, I sped up without thinking, trying to get a closer look at him to determine his overall condition. Why I felt the need to determine his health is beyond me. This caused him to speed up, after an irritated look back. I sped up a little more, thinking I could get a picture of him. The trail turned right as I was fumbling in a pocket for my phone. The coyote made the turn just fine, but I didn't.

I drove directly off the trail and landed in a small gully full of soft powder. Buried. The coyote realized this and stopped to watch me, only to take off once more when Dan came around the trail and slowed, almost certainly rolling his eyes that I was, yet again, stuck. I foolishly pointed down the trail and yelled, "Coyote!" Foolishly, because, faced with the prospect of helping dig me out or going to look at a coyote, he was going to choose the latter with no hesitation. I was on my own with that buried six-hundred-pound snowmobile.

The other incident was at the end of our second day. We were headed back to the cabin but, for some reason that now escapes me, we decided to make a side trip into Caribou. Having ridden in the County now for all of two days, I was confident in my navigation and naively sure I had seen everything it could throw at us. Coming down the trail, I could see the town ahead through some trees but hadn't seen any of the trail signs informing riders to slow, or use caution, or that there was a right-hand turn ahead.

I hadn't seen them because they were all under snow. Normally these signs are nailed to trees and where there aren't trees they sit atop five-foot stakes driven into the ground. That year was such a big snow year that all those stakes were buried. Naturally, none of this occurred to me as I roared down the trail, looking forward to the end of the day, a warm cabin, and a cold beer. I had no idea that I should be cautious here and slow down to a rate of speed reasonable for the imminent turn. At the last second, realizing I had missed a sign or maybe a sign was missing, I let go of the throttle, squeezed the brake, started what would end up being an uncontrolled skid, and finally leapt off the sled as it launched itself off the trail and into another snowbank.

Bewildered and pretty well ticked off, I announced to Dan that maybe they ought to mark the goddamned trails a little better. He calmly pointed back down the trail and I saw, now that I wasn't scooting along at about fifty mph, the very tip of a yellow caution sign. Those trails were all marked just fine. They just happened to be buried in snow and I should have known better. Occasionally, I wonder why I'm so often the sled out front, leading the way. I've come to the conclusion that, for Dan and Jeff, the entertainment value of watching my mishaps is too good to pass up.

> Trail signs inform riders to slow or use caution or that there are turns ahead. Normally these signs are nailed to trees or atop five-foot stakes driven into the ground. In big snow years, though, those signs can be buried under the snow.

Our next trip to the County was in early March 2016. This was the winter that wasn't, as far as snow in Maine goes. It was also the

The Viper after I bailed out. Photo by Danny McGovern.

first year I had the Backcountry, which is assuredly why we didn't get snow. I had only managed to get a few hundred miles on it so far that winter. We had been waiting patiently, kind of, for a good chance to go anywhere there might be snow, and the situation had gotten so desperate that I was contemplating a trip to Canada's Gaspé Peninsula. Luckily, we didn't have to go that far. The computer models were hinting at a big rain coming for the state, except for the County, which would get snow. I called Dan and said I thought we should chance it, that it looked promising but who knew? We loaded up and went.

We stayed in Wallagrass at the Trackdown Kennels and Lodge, a place owned by a Registered Maine Guide and his daughter. They had everything I always look for when I stay overnight in snow country—food, a bar, trails right out the door, lots of parking for our big trailer, and Wi-Fi. Arriving midafternoon, we dropped our sleds off in his parking lot and drove the last few miles along Route 11 into Fort Kent.

Fort Kent is famous for a few things. It's the northern terminus of US Route 1 (with the other end in Key West), and every year at ice-out, crowds gather to watch the massive ice floes coming down the St. John River. Fort Kent hosts the US National Nordic ski races every year as well, and of course Canada is just across the river. It's a stunning piece of Maine with big rolling hills, lakes, ponds, the Fish River, and, we were pleased to see, snow. There was no lack of it.

That evening at the lodge we noted a fleet of Yamaha work sleds with long tracks and extra-wide skis, all with cargo mounts behind the seats and several with rifle cases hard-mounted. The owner informed us that he guided coyote hunting trips and this week's trip was with a group of lobstermen from Down East. These guys were doing the same thing I was—when it's too rough to haul traps or the lobsters just aren't moving, it's time to head north. Their sleds were pretty serious-looking machines and were fun to look at.

Our goal that trip was Estcourt Station. Estcourt Station is a border crossing village in the extreme north of Maine. In fact, you can't get any farther north in Maine without being in Canada. It is a very remote spot, and you have to make sure you get there when the single gas station is open or you'll be stuck for the night. On the American side, during the winter, you can only get there by snowmobile. From Wallagrass, it's a half-hour ride to Fort Kent, and from there ITS 92 takes you along the St. John River to St. Francis and then the town of Allagash, where the Allagash River joins the St. John. From the aptly named Two Rivers Lunch, you can run two or three miles upriver to a small village called Dickey, cross a bridge, and it's here that we assumed the trail to Estcourt Station began. That was about all I knew when we left that morning. Didn't know if it was groomed all the way, didn't know frozen the river was, didn't know of any shortcuts, and was only vaguely aware of the fuel situation.

I wasn't thinking too much about those things because there were sixteen inches of fresh powder on the ground and it was still snowing. The storm, which was producing rain over most of the state, had never been anything but snow in the County and we woke up to a dream come true. Being a Tuesday morning, nobody was out riding, and the groomers hadn't been out either. We had untracked powder all the way to Joe's Country Store, the last fuel stop on the road to Allagash, and never saw anyone until we came across a lone rider headed the opposite way. It was exactly the sort of conditions I had been waiting to try my new Backcountry in and I wasn't disappointed.

If you visit the Allagash, you'd best go to Two Rivers Lunch. And if you have a meal there, you'll be delighted. There are more pictures of hunting and fishing, and more taxidermy mounts, on display here than anywhere else I've been in Maine, including L.L. Bean. Massive bull moose, bobcats, bears, partridge, brook trout, and owls all look over the tables, next to row upon row of photos of successful deer and bear hunts. Even for those who don't hunt or fish, you get the feeling that the untamed North Woods is truly just outside the door. It's one of those places where I come in with a big head of steam, confident and cocky, and by the time I leave I've realized the local guides and woodsmen have forgotten more about the Allagash than I'll ever know, and I'm humbled and awed by it all.

After eating, we got the skinny on the trail to Estcourt from the proprietor. She informed us that it hadn't been groomed but was signed and the local trailmaster had been there and back just a few days before. Furthermore, given that we were coming from Wallagrass, there was a rumor of a local trail crossing the river back in St. Francis that would knock thirty miles off the trip. We were told this freely by the cheerful woman at Two Rivers Lunch. She must have known that if we took the shortcut, she surely wouldn't see us for lunch the next day, but it was more important to her that we had a good experience and good riding.

Fed to repletion, we were off again, through the local deer yards and over the big vehicle bridge at Dickey, where we got turned around by mildly confusing trail signs and a road crossing that seemed to end right in the tarred centerline. After a half-mile jaunt down the side of the road, which is more or less illegal, I saw snow-mobile tracks leading off to the northwest and we realized that we had blundered back onto the trail, although, truth be told, there are so many logging roads and dead ends we weren't entirely sure where we were. By this time, it was nearing two in the afternoon and that put Estcourt out of reach for the day. Oh, sure, we could've gotten there, but we would have been left with one hundred miles back to the lodge and wouldn't have arrived until later that night, possibly missing dinner service.

Trying to get our bearings, I suggested to Dan that we try to find that mystery shortcut trail across the river. If we found that, we would be primed to get to our destination the next day. The storm had finally cleared away to the east, and we had cold, windy riding, delightful with the fresh snow. I could just make out sled tracks from before the storm and so felt reasonably comfortable that I wasn't totally in danger of getting lost. A guide at Two Rivers had told us the shortcut started as a skidder road going east from the Glazier Lake trail and ended as a tiny but marked goat path down to the St.

John. After three dead ends in a row, and with frustration mounting, we stopped and shut off our sleds to regroup. It's always a strange feeling to be sitting in the silence, in the deep woods, and hear nothing but wind and trees creaking and popping.

We were each silently contemplating our dilemma when we heard sleds off in the distance and coming closer by the sound of them. All of a sudden there they were, two Arctic Cats, and the riders pulled up for a chat. They were locals from Madawaska, and when I mentioned what we were looking for, they said they were after the same thing. The lead rider said we were in fact on the right skidder trail, he thought, and off he went to find the goat path. Five minutes later he was back to confirm that it was half a mile away and that our tracks from moments ago had gone right past it twice. I was sure it was nothing but a dead end but seeing as how we didn't have anything better to do, we teamed up and followed them.

Of course, he was right. The trail was marked with the remains of a tattered Hannaford bag tied in the low branches of an alder tree. It looked for all the world like some trash had just gotten stuck in the tree, but on closer inspection, we could just make out the trail, barely a foot path, going down toward the river. It was no wonder Dan and I had missed it. The four of us wound our way down toward the river, finally coming out on the north bank. We could see a mile or so upriver and down, and I watched as the first of our new friends picked his way cautiously, but steadily, across the very frozen river. I was third to go and it was, honestly, exhilarating. I had crossed the St. John! On a snowmobile! Highlight of the winter right there! But I would never have had the guts to do it if we hadn't met up with those Cat riders. We drove up and over the bank on the south side and came out at the back parking lot of Joe's Country

Store, where we fueled up, split ways with the two locals, and found ourselves back on ITS 92. A while after that, we were back at the lodge for a few beers and dinner. We ran into the lobstermen from Down East again and talked fishing, hunting, and riding with them. They were a good bunch of guys who took their pastimes seriously.

Day two of the trip dawned cold—about zero—when we left that morning. The wind had died off a bit during the night. With the promise of a sunny day, we were off. Taking the newfound short-cut across the river to the main trail, we faced some forty miles of trail-breaking to Estcourt. By this time, I was absolutely loving my new sled and its abilities in the deep snow. We bombed along like we had been making the run all our lives. Every few miles, I'd catch a glimpse of a yellow trail sign and the mileage left to Estcourt. It was always a relief to see those signs verifying that we were on the right track. I was still able to see old sled tracks from before the storm, and that helped too. This is truly wild country. Mile after mile of woods, logging roads, hills, and valleys. The whole morning, we saw only one building, and that was a hunting camp stuck out there by itself.

At one point, still with twenty miles to go, we rounded a corner and came face to face with two moose. They were in no hurry to go anywhere, and I certainly wasn't going to go around them on the narrow trail. Late in the winter, moose often use snowmobile trails for traveling as the snow in the woods is too deep. We followed them for nearly a mile as they sauntered along with the awkward gait for which they are so well known. Finally, when it suited their purposes, they disappeared into the woods and we were free to go.

The trail here skirts the shores of Beau Lake, on the American side, and is quite narrow. We could see where drivers of previous sleds had gone down to the lake, maybe to ice fish, or maybe it was the Border Patrol keeping an eye on things. Hard to say, but it was a lonely spot either way.

I was getting a little nervous at this point, as the most recent signs said we still had more than fifteen miles to go and my fuel gauge was below a quarter of a tank. Dan's was reading empty. I figure'd we'd be running on fumes by the time we got to the border. Breaking trail in a foot and a half of new snow wasn't doing my fuel mileage any favors—but it sure was fun.

Five miles from Estcourt, I realized Dan wasn't behind me. I slowed and finally stopped at the end of a long straightaway. After a few minutes of waiting and not hearing him, I realized I was in a bit of a pickle. I was nearly out of gas and assumed Dan had run completely out and was back down the trail waiting for me. I could go back to see what was up, but I would run the risk of running out of gas myself. Or I could continue on into the border town, fuel up my sled, and try to borrow a can of fuel to bring back to Dan. I chose the latter and the fellow at the gas station was happy to lend me a fuel can. I sped back the way I had come and found Dan only a mile or so from where I had first stopped to wait. He had taken a corner a bit too fast, gotten off the side of the trail, and was mired in six feet of snow. He was also not in a good frame of mind. He had been digging by himself and was starting to envision his son-in-law waiting in some restaurant, tucking into a big hot cheeseburger, while he was waist-deep in snow with an overheated Renegade. I explained to him my thought process and he agreed he would have done the same thing. We put the tow rope on and had his sled out in no time, and thirty minutes later we sat down to lunch in Canada.

Getting around in Estcourt Station is strange. Coming in off the trail knowing I had to get back to Dan, I blundered my way through it and got lucky. To get to the gas station, you take a hard right onto a plowed dirt road and follow along a big stream until the road veers over to the US Border Patrol station. Not wanting to run into an issue (I didn't have my passport) and knowing it's better to ask forgiveness than permission sometimes, I turned left just before the station and wound my way through some woods and, miraculously, ended up in the back of the gas station where the fellow loaned me the can of fuel. A short time later Dan and I did this exact same route and happily returned the owner his gas jug. We fueled up, went about one hundred feet and met the Canadian Border Patrol. The agent was quite nice and spoke English with a wonderful accent. She informed us, while looking at each of our licenses, that we would be fine to come into Canada for lunch and wasn't concerned in the slightest when we told her we didn't have passports. On the way back, we stopped at the US Border Patrol station and I have to say the ranger there wasn't too chatty. He looked irritated when we told him that we didn't have passports, and I suspect it's a daily occurrence for him. Who thinks to bring their passports along when they go snowmobiling? Nonetheless, I was full of questions and you'd suspect, in a remote spot like that, he'd have been willing to have a conversation with anyone that happened by. But sometimes my comments aren't taken in the jesting way they are delivered. Maybe he was just fed up with innocent sledders wandering the North Country. We took the hint and moved on.

The ride back was just as much fun and, in some ways, more so. We knew exactly where we were going with no worries about fuel or directions this time. As the afternoon wore on, the temperature dropped, and the wind came up—luckily from the northwest so we had a nice tailwind for the ride home. Halfway back to the St. John

At the cold and remote Estcourt Station. Photo by Danny McGovern.

River, we came across a pack of four sleds stopped at the hunting camp. They wanted to know the distance and condition of the trail to Estcourt, and we were happy to pass on what we had learned. I don't know if they ever made it all the way north, but I don't blame them for their caution. You don't want to hang out in those woods while waiting for help to arrive.

That was the last riding we did that trip. As far as snow was concerned, our timing was perfect. The locals all said it was the best riding of the winter and in fact they were fielding more and more calls about available rooms from other downstaters chasing snow. The word was getting out in snowmobile circles, but Dan and I had really nailed it with the fresh powder. It was the best riding I had ever done—of course, having the new sled helped—and fostered what I know will be a lifelong love of the Allagash.

That particular trip was eye-opening for several reasons besides snowmobiling. I had heard over the years, rather vaguely, about the Can-Am 250. This is an internationally-known sled dog race held every March in Fort Kent. When we were riding there, we saw numerous signs regarding the upcoming event, and on our last night in the lodge I asked the owner about it. After exploring a little bit of the area, I was intrigued. Mulling over the information on the long ride back to Liberty, we hatched a plan to come back the next winter, this time with the family, to watch the race. Mary says it was just an excuse to take yet another snowmobiling trip, but she's only half right.

For Christmas 2016, Dan, Jeff, and I informed our wives we would be taking them to watch the 2017 Can-Am Crown International Sled

Dog Races. This was mostly met with raised eyebrows and snorts of derision, even when we explained all the other fun outdoor activities to do such as skiing and snowshoeing. We had booked three suites at the Inn of Acadia in Madawaska. These were the most modern accommodations we could find in the top of the County and centrally located to trails and restaurants. We stressed the importance of getting out of the house during the long Maine winter. This was, we informed them, going to be a wonderful trip to see a very cool event.

As it turned out, that was a very strange winter, weather-wise. It started off promising, with good riding in December, but January was hot, then cold, then hot again. By hot, I mean temperatures in the fifties, and that *is* hot for a Maine winter. It would snow and then it would turn to rain, then Arctic high pressure would blast down from Canada and freeze it all solid. There were storms, to be sure, but it was a tough year to schedule a trip in advance. You just had to be ready to roll when the snow fell. Nevertheless, we were committed to going and, as March neared, I reminded everyone about it.

"You remember we're going north next week, Mary?"

"How long are you going for?"

"No, I mean all of us. For the sled dog race."

"Oh. That. How far is that place?"

"It's called Fort Kent. It's a three-hour drive."

It's actually more like four and a half hours from Liberty, but I assumed that once we were on the road she wouldn't be inclined to jump out of the truck. The highlight of the drive up for Mary was seeing a red fox run across the road just after Ashland, an event that caused her to shriek with joy and clap her hands. The fox didn't do as much for me, but I took it as a good omen for the overall trip.

As on the trip the year before, about the time we were going through Portage the piles of snow along the road started getting bigger. This did much to improve the overall mood in the truck, as the backseat crew (the in-laws) were starting to eye the beer stashed in the cooler. We got to Fort Kent and took a right toward Madawaska and it started snowing. It didn't amount to much, maybe an inch, but it's always nice to have it snow when you're in snow country.

We got there on a Thursday night. Friday morning, I suggested that it might be nice to go for a quick ride. Ignoring the dark looks from the ladies, who knew full well it would be anything but a quick ride, Dan, Jeff, and I geared up and headed out. I forgot about a trail map but the GPS on my sled was working. It was soon apparent that the snow conditions would prevent any off-trail riding. The County had gotten a rare winter rain earlier that week, naturally followed by an Arctic blast that froze everything to the consistency of white cement. The groomers had all they could do to keep the trails loosened up enough to provide cooling for the sleds.

I had learned that the engine coolant on snowmobiles traveled along the tunnel, over the track, and the snow kicked up by the paddles in turn kept the engine from overheating, acting much like a radiator. If the snow is packed too hard, as it was this particular week, the paddles would have very little snow to throw at the tunnel and the engine would overheat. If a foot of fresh snow had fallen at this point, we would have had near perfect conditions but, alas, it was just cold and icy. We rode around long enough to get hungry for lunch and concluded that, while *any* riding was good riding, this icy stuff left a lot to be desired.

Dan was leading the way back to town when Jeff and I spotted the moose. I had slowed when I saw footprints in the trail, and when we stopped Jeff saw one moose heading away over a small ridge. I saw another that was bedded down about fifty feet off the trail. This animal, a cow, seemed quite ill. Dan had circled back to us and we watched as she struggled, but failed, to stand up. Concluding that she might have brain worm or some other moose disease, we decided to see about finding a game warden who could put her out of her misery.

We sped back to town, called the state police, who passed on the opportunity to shoot a moose out of season, and finally got a game warden to meet us at the Madawaska snowmobile clubhouse, just across Route 1 from the St. John River. We informed him of the situation and condition of the poor animal and he agreed it was likely brain worm. I asked about that and he said it's a bacteria moose get from deer. Deer aren't harmed by it but it's often fatal to moose. He unloaded his sled by backing it straight off the end of his truck, where it crashed to the ground (I could just hear Dan snorting about that being a page out of my playbook) and started gearing up for the short ride. I was full of questions about the staggering amount of gear in the cab of his truck, offering at one point to carry his shotgun out to the site if that would be helpful. It wouldn't be, turns out, although I think he at least got that I was joking (I wasn't).

Fifteen minutes later, we were back with the sick animal. The warden drove his sled off the trail to within ten feet from the moose, shut it off, and walked over. He fired two quick shots that echoed through the little valley. The three of us walked in for a closer look. It was sad. The moose's overall condition appeared perfect, but we could see the marks in the snow where she had struggled, unsuccessfully, to stand. We told the warden about the other smaller moose Jeff had seen running off, and he suggested it may have been the yearling of the cow he had just put down.

I asked him about the meat. I mean, really, there were three hundred pounds of fresh moose steaks lying in front of us. Have you ever had moose meat chili? It's delicious. Unfortunately, he recommended we not eat any and that he would call some locals to see if they wanted it for coyote bait. Friends of mine have since suggested to me that I should have ignored his advice and at least taken the back straps . . . but I submit that if they had seen that poor girl suffering they wouldn't have risked going out the same way.

The only funny thing about this day belonged to Jeff. He has ridden sleds longer than I have, although maybe not as religiously, and yet somehow had never come across a moose. That night at dinner we were relating the day's events and he said, "All these years looking for a moose and never seeing one. Now today we see one and what happens? We have to shoot it!"

Sick moose aside, and contrary to Mary's suspicions, we were there to see sled dogs. The next morning was the scheduled start of the three different events that make up the Can-Am, a thirty-miler, a hundred-miler, and the epic 250-mile race. We had to be in Fort Kent by eight if we wanted to see the start of the first one, the thirty-miler. But it was cold! The temperature at the hotel was eight below zero and there was twenty mph of northwest wind pushing it around.

It may sound strange, but I had trouble that morning deciding what to wear. I mean, did I want to don my full riding gear? It would certainly be warm enough, but kind of bulky to walk around in. Shoes or boots? I finally decided to err on the side of caution and comfort, and went with some of the riding gear. I should have worn it all, including my helmet. We got to the start of the race to find that the organizers had spent all night lining Main Street with a two-foot-deep by eight-foot-wide swath of snow.

We were in time to see the first team get launched from the

A team departing Fort Kent for the hundred-miler.

starting gate. If you've never been to see sled dogs, you are in for a treat. We were all amazed by the energy those dogs have. Clearly all they want to do is run. And they're small. I was expecting to see big Siberian huskies or malamutes, not these slender guys. They were maybe forty pounds and all bone and sinew. After talking with a few of the veterinarians who work for the event, I can see the logic. They don't eat as much so the musher doesn't have to carry as much food, and their diminutive size means their bodies don't take the pounding a heavier dog would suffer on the grueling trail.

We watched all the teams take off, then went in to warm up. Every year the local car dealership opens up its showroom to be used as a massive warming hut, and everyone there was glad of it. There were huge vats of hot chocolate and coffee, fresh doughnuts and hot dogs, pots of chili and platters of cookies, all provided by the sponsors of the race. I got to chatting with someone about it all and was surprised to learn that the main race, the 250, was a qualifier for the Iditarod in Alaska.

After the first round of teams had sped off, we walked up Main Street, looking at the bridge to Canada and the marker for the beginning of Route 1. I picked up one of the canvas booties the dogs wear to protect their feet. I frowned to myself, thinking of the abuse the animal's foot might take without it. I saved this bootie for one of my nephews who happens to love dog sledding—he's still got it.

We spent the rest of the morning going back and forth between the dealership and the starting line, and after all the teams were out of the gate we headed across town to the finish line at the Lonesome Pine Trails ski lodge. It wasn't long before the teams started running in, and what a sight to see them coming across the bottom of the ski trails! The dogs didn't appear the least bit tired as they were inspected, one team at a time, by the vets. Some of the mushers were happy and some frustrated, but none seemed perturbed by the cold. One sled had broken some struts after hitting a tree on the route; it was lashed back together with the musher's ax and some rope.

We were all stunned to see one young musher come in with no hat of any kind, and another who appeared better dressed for a morning jog in the suburbs. They are truly a unique bunch of people, and they had my admiration. It must really be something to be out in those big woods with just a sled and the dog team in front pulling. Each musher, as they crossed the finish line, went immediately to check on the welfare of the dogs. We were all happy to see the devotion the mushers have to their animals.

Back in Madawaska that night, I thought everyone was duly impressed with the day, even though it was the coldest weather anyone could remember. It's a very popular, and very important, event for northern Maine. I urge anyone in southern Maine to make the trip some year. You won't be sorry. I have since learned that when the races are over (the 250-miler doesn't finish for two more days), many of the locals go and ride the race route on their snowmobiles. This is an eagerly awaited chance to ride in some of the more remote spots in the Allagash, as the trail has been well-packed by the teams and explores some of the wilder regions of the area. One of these years I hope to do the same.

This particular trip was one that I had told quite a few friends and neighbors about in the preceding months, and they all were eager to hear about it when we returned. Usually I get just one or two questions about where I went and how cold it was when I got there, but people seemed genuinely interested in the County and dog sledding. I believe the County has that effect on many people. It has a mystique about it that is hard to describe. I suppose in some ways it reminds me of my own home. I've spent more than two decades on a sparsely inhabited island, and remoteness doesn't bother me in the least, but every summer I get asked a thousand times, "What's it like here in the winter?" The answer I give is the same answer I suspect you'd get from someone in Aroostook County: "It's wonderful."

◆ Recommended Ride

If you ride in the County, it won't be too many miles before you come across a sign indicating the mileage and direction to a place called the Lakeview. Located just south of Madawaska, in the small town of St. Agatha, the Lakeview Restaurant and Campground is an institution in these parts. Dan had told us all about it back home, and on my first trip to ride out of Caribou we found our way there on the first day. We pulled into the parking lot, and row upon row of snowmobiles were all neatly parked with their noses facing the wind. We shut our sleds down and, I admit, looking out at all those sleds, I felt a pang of sadness for my little Viper. She seemed outclassed by the fancy new machines, but the more I looked around I realized that wasn't quite the case. Upon closer inspection, I realized there were sleds older, in some cases much older, than the ones Dan and I were riding. We clomped in the front door and found a long row of jackets and helmets, hung ours alongside them, and found our way to the big bar in the middle of the restaurant. I was learning that everyone in the County, it seems, rides snowmobiles, and half of them were here for lunch. That day we talked with people from all over Maine and New England, a couple from Tennessee, another from Pennsylvania, all of them here to ride the best trails around and have lunch overlooking Long Lake. Everyone was relaxed, laughing and joking, and eavesdropping. I could tell that no one wanted to go back home. Why would they?

7

Lessons Learned

Snowmobiling isn't always fun.

Mary and I headed north from Liberty on a February afternoon several years ago, the day after attending a 1,500-person beer festival in Portland. It was also the day after an ugly storm system had crossed the region, dropping an inch of rain on the entire state. This was one of those storms the weather guys refer to as an "inside runner," meaning that the energy and moisture involved with the storm runs to the west of the state, drawing in warm southerly flow and all but assuring rain instead of snow.

On social media, much was made of this particular storm. The snowmobile clubs all knew it was coming, and they all knew the potential for damaged trails. I knew the storm was coming and also that the riding wasn't going to be great after it left, but we were committed. For Christmas Mary had booked us on a couple's ride. We would depart The Forks, take a seventy-five-mile ride, and arrive in Kingfield by the southern route. There we would have dinner and stay the night at the Herbert Grand, the big hotel in town, and the next morning ride the northern route back to The Forks. I was thrilled when I opened this present and read the voucher, complete with ITS trail numbers, mileage, and names of towns I'd been

Our little cabin.

through already and some I'd been waiting for. Mary was going to be using Dan's new Polaris and seemed genuinely interested, if not quite exuberant, about the prospect of the trip.

We arrived at The Forks around five that afternoon after a generally quiet and cold ride up 201. Naturally the temperature had plummeted after the storm swept through, and now everything was in the process of freezing solid. Typical. We made one stop in Bingham to get a new helmet for Mary. Before leaving Liberty that afternoon she had tried on a few of the older versions that were kicking around until I realized, a bit shamefaced, that this was my *wife*! And I should probably spring for a new helmet. I've never thought of myself as being cheap and I wasn't here either. Just daft.

We noticed more snow the farther north we got and that was some encouragement to us, but I had my doubts. It had just been too warm, for too long, and it would only take a few yahoos out tearing around on soft trails before the refreeze would ruin everything. Still, over beers and dinner at the Northern Outdoors lodge, we chatted with a few folks and all reports were better than I expected. Maybe it wouldn't be so bad after all. It helped that attached to the main building was one of the older breweries in Maine, Kennebec River Brewery, still going strong since 1996. I recommend a beer called "Sledhead Red," by the way. Great name.

The next morning dawned cold. Six below zero at our little cabin, and we were in no particular rush to get going. After a leisurely breakfast and second cup of coffee, I told Mary I'd go warm up and fuel up our sleds while she finished a few emails. I was mostly geared up, wearing a winter hat instead of my helmet since I'd just be idling around the compound for a while. Unlatching the front of the trailer door, I gave a nonchalant pull on the handle, expecting the forward ramp to swing down. Instead I got spun around as my arm seemed to come half out of its socket. The ramp, still in the upright and closed position, hadn't moved. Upon closer inspection, I realized it was frozen shut. I could see the frost crystals on the gasket. I pounded on it, thinking I could break the frost with a few well-placed thumps of my fist, but to no avail.

Walking around the trailer I stepped in through the side door, walked forward to the frozen ramp door, and lowered my shoulder. *Boom!* Nothing. *Boom, boom!* Nothing. Turning around I placed my hands on the cowling of my Ski-Doo, craned my neck around, selected my target, and slammed my heavily booted foot into the edge of the ramp. *Bam!* Nothing. *Bam, bam, bam!* I realized that I was again in a situation common to my snowmobiling escapades. Anyone walking by, or even driving by, would be looking at the trailer, wondering who was in it and, more importantly, what the issue was. *Is he stuck in there? Is it even a human? What's that snarling noise?*

I gave up finally, thinking I should add a generator and heat gun to the list of things we bring riding. The beauty of our new three-place trailer is that there are two means of egress for sleds, and I could back them out of the rear door if that front door wouldn't open. Most experienced riders, at this point, may very well be yelling, "Don't do it, you knucklehead." I wish they had been there to force the point home. I started my sled, pleased as ever with its ability in cold weather, and moved back to Dan's Polaris. It fired right up, so I hopped off and exited quickly, as two-stroke engine smoke filled the trailer.

I opened the back ramp and the smoke rolled out as I walked back in and sat on Dan's sled, thinking I'd back it out in a jiffy. Hitting the button to reverse the engine, I squeezed the throttle, the engine coughed (I was already coughing), and then it died. I repeated the process, and it died again. On the third try, as I was realizing I needed to get fresh air or perish, the snowmobile lurched backward and slid out and down the ramp. Looking back on it with a clearer mind, I suspect it could only have resembled some kind of massive industrial bong hit, as the trailer first took in a form of energy (me), shook its massive square body in pleasure, and then expelled a giant cloud of smoke, complete with sled and rider.

After pulling in breath after breath of clean, cold northern Maine air, I felt somewhat revived. I went back in, backed the Ski-Doo out, and went off to fuel them both up, thankful today's snowmobile issue was over and we could get on to some riding. I drove the Back-country across the compound and asked the fellow at the pumps if he would top it off while I went back after the Polaris. While driving Dan's sled over, I noticed it bogging down several times, and then it stalled right as I got to the pump.

"Kinda cold-blooded, huh?"

"Yah, it's my father-in-law's. Don't know anything about these."

"Well, maybe it just needs to warm up."

After filling up both sleds, I brought them back to the cabin. My sled was fine, but Dan's had what I'd call serious hesitation. It would idle just fine but give it a little gas and it would go twenty feet and bog down. I took the cowling off, thinking I would replace the spark plugs, but I couldn't find any new spares. After swearing for ten minutes, I managed to get the cowling back on and went inside for my helmet, thinking that running down the trail might "blow out" whatever was causing the issue.

Of course, no such thing happened. I managed to get the sput-tering sled just out of sight of the lodge, where the engine promptly died. I restarted it and lurched another hundred feet before it died again. I realized our morning was officially shot. Twenty minutes later, I had the ailing snowmobile perched in the bed of my truck and was on my way up Route 201 to Jackman Powersports. Mary had watched a few of my antics from the cabin but had long since resumed work on her laptop.

If snowmobilers make a pilgrimage to Jackman, then its shrine must be Jackman Powersports. They sell and service all four makes of snowmobiles, have a massive snowmobile storage facility, and are likely responsible for keeping more sleds on the trails than any other business in Maine. The owner is a touch on the grumpy side, I'll admit, but he once referred to me as "young fella" and that seemed like it could have been a lot worse. I left the sled in the capable hands of his mechanics and continued through and then north out of town on 201. I had ridden sleds to the border but had never driven a vehicle here. It was the last sixteen miles of Route 201 that I had never been on and it is a stunning ride. After Dennistown and Spruce Meadow Cabins, the road winds upward. Sandy Stream Mountain is on the left, with Slidedown Mountain a bit farther west, and looking to the east you can see Boundary Bald Mountain. With a classic tumbling stream alongside the road for a while it becomes nearly impossible to stay in your own lane. In fact, 201 here is very similar to driving through one of the notches in the White Mountains; it's almost identical terrain. Turning around at the border crossing (no passport or I might have kept right on going), I pulled off onto a plowed dirt road, thinking I might as well scout for future trips. I poked around for a while, coming across a few locales with names I recognized and a couple of maple sugaring outfits, and then popped back out to 201 and blasted back into town. The mechanic was just bringing Dan's sled out when I pulled in and I asked him what the problem had been.

"Your clutch faces were froze up."

"Oh, man! The clutch faces?"

"Yup. Should be fine now."

Sled issues, weather issues, health issues—you name it and we had issues.

I of course had no idea that clutches had faces, but I was glad he had them thawed out. It occurred to me that the moisture from the rainstorm was causing us several issues—first the frozen door on the trailer and now this. I was soon on my way back down 201, after having picked up a spare set of spark plugs just in case, and Mary and I were blasting our way out of the lodge compound by one o'clock.

By one-thirty we were creeping along the trail, gingerly picking our way through huge ruts, the skis making jarring scratches in the now-frozen slush, finding out for ourselves just how much other damage the rainstorm had done. There was no bare ground anywhere, but where the rain had swollen streams they had flooded their banks until they poured out onto the trails, and a day later the cold air had frozen them solid. Where the trail had gotten soft, you could see where a sled had come barreling through, leaving a trench of slush in its wake, and then all *that* had frozen solid. This went on, in different places, for as much as half a mile. It was miserable.

Both snowmobiles overheated, and while we were stopped to let them cool down, I told Mary that if the trails didn't get better up near Coburn Mountain I thought we should turn back. I was afraid we were going to do serious damage to the sleds by running them across all this frozen muck. I felt the need to apologize to Mary, and when I did she asked why. I explained that normally these trails would be flat, all snow, and a ton of fun to ride.

We crossed 201, rode along the river for a while and climbed ever upward, but to no avail. After hitting another long stretch of frozen, trenched slush, I turned us around.

"Sorry, hon. It's no good."

"Well, it's your call. I'm kind of cold anyway."

"Let's just go back to the cabin and call it a day."

We weren't far from the lodge, maybe fifteen miles. Normally this would take no longer than twenty-five or thirty minutes, but with the trails in the shape they were in, it was well over an hour before we finally pulled up to our cabin. And we were cold. The temperature had never gotten out of the single digits, and the riding had us both chilled.

I noticed I was also more tired than I should have been, and my throat was raw from coughing in the smoke-filled trailer that morning. After a time, Mary had her feet warmed up and was contemplating a glass of wine, but I was still shivering. I shivered all through dinner, and it slowly dawned on me that I was getting sick. The next morning, Mary packed up the cabin while I feverishly hooked onto the trailer with the truck and soon we were headed south on 201.

Almost nothing had gone right on this trip. Sled issues, weather issues, health issues—you name it and we had issues. Sometimes this is just how snowmobiling goes, and it's a good metaphor for life. A friend who happens to share my love of tuna fishing often says you have to go out on the rough days to truly appreciate the calm days. He's right, of course, and this isn't limited to fishing. The trip couldn't have gone much worse for Mary and me, but we were together in the North Country and that's what mattered.

The Next Ride

When folks ask me about my latest trip, I'm happy to discuss where it was, snow depth, temperature, the animals we came across, the price of fuel, and where we had lunch. Yet, as soon as one trip ends I'm often considering the next on the list. It's a long list. Friends ask where my favorite place to snowmobile is, and that's a tough question.

The answer is that there is no clear winner. I've had great rides everywhere I've been. Mostly it comes down to conditions. The last ride from Liberty in 2017 was one of the best I had all year and certainly the warmest. Kole tagged along for the afternoon and we rode from the farmhouse to Frye Mountain and on into the Thorndike area. There was plenty of snow coverage and the lakes were frozen solid, and on that mid-March morning the sun came out to stay, the temperature neared fifty degrees, and we found ourselves riding in sweatshirts. That was a first for me and it felt great to not be wearing twenty-five pounds of clothes.

Every fall, I keep a running list in my head of must-do rides. I like starting in Oquossoc, but I'm not beholden to it. This year Libby Camps and the Shin Pond area are frontrunners, and the trains will be a good goal for that ride. Left on a spit of land between Chamberlain and Eagle Lakes, far from any roads, these two steam locomotives are leftovers from a bygone era. They are massive, and on most riders' bucket list. I also have been thinking about riding around the Milo area, maybe with a jaunt down toward Old Town. It might be kind of fun to find that trail at the bottom of our old Stillwater house. The Deboullie Loop Trail, in the Allagash, is wonderful, and it won't take much convincing for me to go back to that part of Maine.

Then I realize I never did get around to the Sunrise Trail, from Ellsworth to Machias, and that suddenly becomes a necessity. Jackman always beckons, although the last two years I have enjoyed riding there later in the season. Then there's Mapleton; some of the boys who grow grain for our breweries ride sleds and we thought it would be fun to pull in on our sleds and check out their operation.

This year, after the Super Bowl, we'll be at Steve's camp again. We've tended to ride north from Sysladobsis, for no particular reason, and now I'd like to go the other way.

I also want to keep learning the trails around the farmhouse in Liberty. I've recently joined the local club, the Frye Mountain Sno-Riders, and I'm looking forward to broadening my knowledge of the local ridges and valleys. So, I've got a busy winter coming up and I hope you do too. See you on the trails and stay right!

Resources

Ten Free Tips for Riding

As you have probably figured out by now, I came to snowmobiling in a roundabout fashion that certainly didn't include much in the way of official training. I have managed to pick up a few tricks along the way, and I include them here so that you can skip having to come upon them yourself the hard way.

1. Overdress, every time. It's winter, it's Maine, and the sun doesn't get too high if it comes out at all. You can always take clothing off but you can't put it on if you didn't bring it.
2. Start dry and stay dry. Nothing will get your skin colder and make your central heating system work harder than trying keep your hands warm in wet gloves or drying your socks out while they're shoved into your still-wet Muck Boots.
3. Tell someone where you are going if you go alone. Leave a note on your truck dashboard, send a text, leave a wooden arrow in the crotch of a tree, whatever you want. If (or when) you break down forty-six miles into the woods, you'll be glad someone came looking and they'll be glad to know which way you went.
4. Know your limits. If it's your first time, don't feel like you have to see how long you can hold the throttle wide open. Oh, I know it's fun—but there's plenty of time for that sort of thing later.
5. Don't follow other people's tracks if it looks sketchy. One of two things will happen—you'll end up following some amateur from Alabama who's already in there, waiting for a tow. Or, that guy who left that track going up that mountain is a *much* better rider than you and will end up towing *you* out.

6. Don't bother if the conditions look cruddy at best. Maybe there's not much snow cover, maybe there are too many ruts in the tracks, maybe the ground's not frozen yet, or maybe it's too icy. If it doesn't look like fun, it probably won't be. Save your time and gas money for after the next storm.

7. Look, it ain't cheap. There's no way around it. So, start reasonably. Unless you're the starting quarterback for the local NFL team, don't break the bank getting all snazzed up with matching gear on your new long-track mountain sled if you're just thinking of towing the kids around the backyard on Sunday mornings. To note: If the kids take a liking to the snowmobile, you're in real trouble.

8. Take a friend, or five. There's always someplace to go, and you can usually find a great spot by a lake, or a lodge with a killer chili recipe, or both. Snowmobiling is much better than cleaning your house on a day off from work.

9. Talk to the people you meet where you go. Mainers are known for their taciturn nature, and rightfully so, but I've found that most of them, when asked, will give you a five-minute answer to a one-minute question, and you'll ride away chuckling to yourself in appreciation of that wit, or pondering their opinion on wind power, or considering the current status of Maine's moose population. It's not always easy to strike up a conversation with someone, even if you're both Mainers, but I find it's always worth it.

10. If you like riding and want it to be something you do every winter, join a club. Riding wouldn't exist without the snowmobile clubs. Go to a meeting. Carry a little bow saw. Help work on a bridge some fall weekend. It matters.

Know the Laws

Alcohol

It's the law: no drinking and riding. If you're over twenty-one, 0.08 percent or more blood alcohol concentration means you are under the influence. If you are under twenty-one, no amount of alcohol in the blood is permitted. During the 2018-19 season, ten people died in snowmobiling accidents. According to the Maine Warden Service, almost half of all crashes, including nonfatal ones, involve alcohol. Just don't do it. It's not worth it.

Accident Reporting

The sad truth is that every year, accidents happen on the trails. Speed, alcohol, inexperience, poor visibility, and not knowing the laws all contribute. If you do have an accident, you are required to report it, whether it involves injury to a person or property. Property damage of $1,000 or more must be reported within seventy-two hours. You can find accident report forms online at www.maine.gov/ifw/atv-snowmobile/snowmobile/.

If it's an emergency, call 911! You can also contact the Maine Warden Service. To reach a game warden twenty-four hours a day, call a dispatch center (but remember, many snowmobile trails are in remote areas with no cell service so be prepared to handle emergencies yourself):

Augusta 1-800-452-4664
Bangor 1-800-432-7381
Houlton 1-800-924-2261

Registration

You don't need an operator's license, but you do need to register your sled. All snowmobiles—from Maine or from out of state—must be registered and renewed annually. Maine residents can register sleds in Augusta or through a registration agent, and can renew online: www.maine.gov/ifw/atv-snowmobile/snowmobile/.

Wardens do run regular checkpoints to keep a lid on alcohol violations and unregistered sleds. A portion of these fees goes to local snowmobile clubs to help groom trails, so it's a win-win.

Check the Ice

Crossing a lake or river can be exhilarating, but don't get fooled. As many as a quarter of all snowmobile accidents come from breaking through ice. For clear blue ice on a lake, you need a thickness of five inches, and more on a river. It's harder to gauge ice safety and spot hazards (like a random ice shack) at night, so go even slower in the dark. Don't ride alone and consider carrying ice picks if you know your route involves a lake or river crossing.

Rent a Sled

Don't have a sled, gear, or experience but can't wait to try it? For the novice rider, whether you've never been or only been a few times, I recommend renting a sled from one of the sled rental outfits scattered across Maine. Most of the bigger towns in snow country—Rangeley, Stratton, Bingham, The Forks, Greenville, Jackman, Millinocket, Caribou, and Fort Kent—have a business that will rent you a wonderful snowmobile for a day, usually for around $200 to $250, a bit more if you need a helmet and warm coat. They are often trail sleds, often very new, and often powered by four-stroke motors.

These are quieter and less smoky. These folks set you up for success. You're given a twenty-minute tutorial, a map of the local trails, a smoothly idling sled with a full tank of gas, and a couple of places to take your kid and their selfie stick.

This is a select list, arranged alphabetically by town, of some of Maine's snowmobile rental outfits. The state certifies agencies to rent snowmobiles for recreational purposes, so you can check online at www.maine.gov/ifw/atv-snowmobile/snowmobile/.

Bingham
North Country Rivers
www.northcountryrivers.com

201 Power Sports
www.201powersports.com

Caratunk
Maine Outdoor Sports
www.maineoutdoorsports.com

Fryeburg
Northeast Snowmobile Rentals
www.northeastsnowmobile.com

Greenville
Northwoods Outfitters
www.maineoutfitter.com

Millinocket
New England Outdoor Center
www.neoc.com

Mount Chase
Shin Pond Village
www.shinpond.com

Presque Isle
The Sled Shop
www.thesledshopinc.com

Rockwood
Moosehead Sled Repair & Rental
www.mooseheadsled.com

The Birches Resort
www.birches.com

Stratton
Flagstaff Rentals
www.flagstaffrentalsmaine.com

The Forks
Northern Outdoors
www.northernoutdoors.com/maine/snowmobile-tours

Get a Guide

If you're not ready to rent a sled and strike out on your own, take a guided tour. There are plenty of places where you can book a tour. This is a select list of outfitters, arranged alphabetically by town. The Maine Snowmobile Association also has a list of rental and guide services; find them online at www.mesnow.com.

Allagash
Allagash Guide Service
www.allagashguideservice.com

Bingham
North Country Rivers
www.northcountryrivers.com

201 Power Sports
www.201powersports.com

Caratunk
Maine Outdoor Sports
www.maineoutdoorsports.com

Greenville
Northwoods Outfitters
www.maineoutfitter.com

Fryeburg
Northeast Snowmobile Rentals
www.northeastsnowmobile.com

Millinocket
New England Outdoor Center
www.neoc.com

Newry
Newry Trails
www.newrytrailsguideservice.com

Portage
Hewes Brook Lodge
www.hewesbrooklodge.com

Stratton
Flagstaff Rentals
www.flagstaffrentalsmaine.com

The Forks
Northern Outdoors
www.northernoutdoors.com/maine/snowmobile-tours

Additional Resources

Maine Snowmobile Association
www.mesnow.com
News, clubs, trail reports, conditions, state laws, trip planning, and chambers of commerce.

There are more than 250 snowmobile clubs in the state; the Maine Snowmobile Association keeps a list, organized by town, of all the clubs affiliated with the MSA.

The Maine Atlas and Gazetteer
Available at www.garmin.com/en-us/
Indispensable for traveling any road in Maine

Maine Advocates for Responsible Backcountry
www.mainearb.com
Nonprofit snowmobile club dedicated to the preservation of, and responsible riding in, Maine's backcountry

National Weather Service
Gray: www.weather.gov/gyx
Caribou: www.weather.gov/car/
Comprehensive weather forecasts, hazards, radar, conditions

Acknowledgments

This book took me two years to write. Actually, it took me two winters. I blasted out seventy-five percent of it the first winter, in between days on the water and days on my sled. The second winter, I finished the rough draft and shanghaied my mother, Judith Ponturo Weber, into helping me edit it. We spent hours on the phone, going through page by page, chasing misspellings, and trying to make it as readable as possible. Only time will tell if we were successful, and I hope she enjoyed the process as much as I did.

I would like to extend my deep thanks to Mia Boynton, Monhegan's librarian, who answered the phone one December afternoon to hear a distraught neighbor pleading for help about some manuscript he lost in his own house. Upon digging deeper into the issue, she calmly found the entire book in the depths of my laptop, restored it to its usual spot, and gave me a free twenty-minute lesson on the proper use of computers in general, and how to save one's work in particular.

Eric Hall of Dennistown has been more helpful to my riding experiences over the years than he is aware of. I'm sure he's about had it with my endless questions, but he politely keeps answering. He still hasn't told me any of his best shortcuts. Brian and Josh, of Chase Toys in Unity, have also answered countless questions. Their honesty and knowledge of the industry are second to none. Steve Keene has been beyond generous, inviting us to ride out of his camp every year. I would have discovered riding in eastern Maine eventually, but he sure made it easy, and fun. As for my comrades-in-arms, Lucas, Kole, Eben, Jeff, James—probably their wives all groan when the phone rings just before a big storm, but I sure am glad these guys keep answering.

Certainly, my father-in-law had no idea what would happen when I first spotted the old snowmobile trailer behind his woodshed, and I hope he's pleased with the way it's all turned out. Of all the people I drag to the out-of-the-way corners of Maine, no one has been with me more than Dan. I can be moody, bossy, and impatient, as well as capable of wonderfully uncomfortable temper tantrums, but Dan's gotten used to dealing with my BS. He's also a busy guy—sometimes it's a trick to get him out of his Lake St. George brewery—but with modern technology he's learned it's possible to order malt and hops from nearly any trail in the state. I hope he's had as much fun as I have.